Marc Kielburger
Craig Kielburger
Deepa Shankaran

THOMSON
—✳—™
NELSON

Australia   Canada   Mexico   Singapore   Spain   United Kingdom   United States

THOMSON

™

NELSON

Take More Action

by Marc Kielburger, Craig Kielburger,
and Deepa Shankaran

Director of Publishing:
David Steele

**Executive Managing Editor,
Development:**
Cheryl Turner

Program Manager:
Nancy Christoffer

Editorial Assistants:
Christi Davis, Charlotte Martin

**Executive Managing Editor,
Production:**
Nicola Balfour

Copy Editor and Proofreader:
Kathy Evans

Senior Production Co-ordinator:
Bev Crann

Creative Director:
Angela Cluer

Interior Design:
Pronk&Associates;
Katherine Strain/Nelson

Cover Design:
Pronk&Associates

Cover Image:
Rob Colvin/The Stock
  Illustration Source

Back Cover Image:
Steve Somerville/York Region
  Newspaper Group

Compositor:
Susan Calverley

Permissions/Photo Researcher:
Indu Ghuman

Printer:
Transcontinental Printing Inc.

Consultants:
Patrick Clarke
British Columbia Teachers'
  Federation

Marc Keirstead
York Catholic District School Board

Tom Kolin
Toronto District School Board

Kit Krieger
West Vancouver Teachers'
  Association

Gregory D. Rogers
Toronto Catholic District School
  Board

Bryan J. Smith
Thames Valley District School
  Board

Claudia Viviani
School District 45, British Columbia

Printed and bound in Canada
1 2 3 4 5 08 07 06 05 04

For more information contact
Nelson, 1120 Birchmount Road,
Toronto, Ontario, M1K 5G4. Or
you can visit our Internet site at
http://www.nelson.com

Photo Credits:

Thanks are due to the following
authors, publishers, and agents for
permission to use the material
indicated:

p. vi: Steve Somerville/York Region
Newspaper Group; **p. 2:** Shaun
Walker/AP/CP Picture Archive;
p. 11: CP Picture Archive;
p. 15: Trstr/CP Picture Archive;
p. 20: © David Young-Wolff/Photo
Edit; **p. 21:** Brennan Linsley/AP/CP
Picture Archive; **p. 23:** © Bettmann/
CORBIS/ MAGMA; **p. 50:** PhotoDisc/
Getty Images; **p. 95:** © Bill Aron/
Photo Edit; **p. 141:** © Chip
Henderson/Index Stock Imagery.

**National Library of Canada
Cataloguing in Publication Data**

Kielburger, Marc
   Take more action / Marc
Kielburger, Craig Kielburger,
Deepa Shankaran.

Includes bibliographical references
ISBN 0-7715-8035-5

1. World citizenship. 2. Social
action. 3. Social advocacy.
4. Young volunteers. 5. Youth—
Political activity. I. Kielburger,
Craig, 1982- II. Shankaran, Deepa
III. Title.

JZ1320.4.K53 2004   323'.042
C2004-900465-4

CONTENTS

Acknowledgments

We would like to thank everyone who helped to make this book a reality, especially all of the young people across Canada and the United States who provided insight and guidance toward making this text a powerful source of social change.

A special word of gratitude goes to Deepa Shankaran, who brought so much passion and commitment to the project for more than a year. We could not have done it without you, Deepa! Many thanks as well to Ed "the fun guy" Gillis for his help, vision, and dedication. Thanks also goes to Roxanne Joyal for her unwavering support over the past eight years; Eva and Yoel Haller for all their love; Lekha Singh for her guidance; Virginia Benderly for her passion; John Gaither for his thousands of hours spent volunteering; and Jaime Forsythe for her excellent research.

We would like to thank everyone at Nelson who helped to make this project a reality, including Greg Pilon, Mike Czukar, Paul Masson, and Patricia Willis. A huge thank-you to the editor extraordinaire, Nancy Christoffer, for all of her efforts. Thanks also goes to Chris Besse and Janice Schoening, formally of Gage Learning, for their help in establishing the *Take Action!* series. Many thanks also to our educational consultants.

Our work would not be possible without the help of Free the Children supporters and members of the Board of Directors, both in Canada and in the United States, and the Free the Children and Leaders Today team, including Lloyd Hanoman, Dalal Al-Waheidi, Victor Li, Antoeneta Popa, Charlotte Sobolewski, Erin Barton, Alex Apostol, Jocelyn Sweet, Peter Ruhiu, Renée Hodgkinson, Bartek Kosinski, Danielle Hoegy, and Chris Delany.

We would like to say a special thank-you to the Toronto District School Board officials who took a chance on the *Take Action!* series, especially David Reid, Gerri Connelly, Allan Hux, Mark Lowry, and Donna Cansfield. Thanks also goes to Isabel Grant from the Vancouver School Board, Greg Rogers and John Ryall from the Toronto Catholic District School Board, Nancy Di Gregorio from the Hamilton Catholic District School Board, and Maureen Dockendorf from the Coquitlam School Board.

Our gratitude goes to the organizations and individuals who believe in our important mission. In this respect, we include Oprah Winfrey, Katy Davis, and Caren Yanis, from the Angel Network, David Krieger and The Nuclear Age Peace Foundation, Leonard Kurz and The Kurz Family Foundation, The i2 Foundation, The Singh Foundation, Buzz Hargrove and the Canadian Auto Workers, The Illinois State Math and Science Academy, Linda Rosier and the team at Concept 3 Advertising Group, Elaine Silver, the Weiss Family, the Apostolopoulos Family, the Joyal Family, and the Heimark Family.

Our family deserves a heartfelt thank-you, including our Mimi, who remains our biggest fan. Finally, and most importantly, we would not be where we are without the love and continuous support of our parents, Fred and Theresa Kielburger. Thank you for everything, Mom and Dad — we love you!

A Message From Marc and Craig Kielburger

For nearly a decade, the young people of Free the Children and Leaders Today have been passionately engaged in changing the world through volunteerism and the movement for social justice. Reaching out to people around the globe to work for a common purpose has taught us many important lessons. Through this book and the *Take Action!* series, we hope to share those lessons with you.

Craig (left) and Marc (right)

Not long ago, we led a group of young volunteers into the Andes Mountains in Ecuador to help construct a school for a rural community. We were excited about the experience and the opportunity to share our resources with our new friends. Yet when we discovered what a challenge it would be to build the school with our own hands, we began to doubt our ability to complete the construction in time.

The elders of the community, however, reassured us that it was possible. They taught us about the *minga*, a tradition of the Puruhae indigenous people that has survived for hundreds of years. It meant that, although this single community would be the only one to benefit from the school, hundreds of people from all over the region would come together to make it stand. Elderly women carried bags of cement to lay the foundation; children who would never be able to attend the school helped to put up the walls of its new classrooms; farmers gave up three precious days at the peak of the growing season to make sure that the job got done. When we asked what moved them to make such sacrifices even though they had nothing to gain from the project, they told us that some things are sacred, and among them are children and education. Values like these proved to be the greatest resource of a people with few possessions, because they united them through all challenges and times. Working alongside this community put our own struggles into context. It taught us that we are all part of something larger than our individual lives, and that our well-being is connected to that of others.

In this guide to social involvement, you will discover what it means and what it takes to be a global citizen. You will learn how to break down and tackle even the most difficult social problems, and how to channel your passion for a better world into concrete actions — big and small. You will also begin to develop and hone the skills that will make your vision clearer and your actions speak louder, and discover how other young people, just like you, are taking up the challenge of confronting injustice in thoughtful, creative ways.

When dealing with tough issues by yourself, it is easy to feel powerless and alone. But as an African proverb holds, "When spider webs unite, they can tie up a lion." When we come together as a *minga* — as citizens of a global community — we can tie up the roots of injustice and secure a happier, more sustainable world. This consciousness and solidarity begins with us, with youth. We are the generation that we have been waiting for. Let's get started!

Global Citizenship: Around the World, Across the Street

C O N T E N T S

The Era of the Global Citizen

Julia Butterfly Hill sat 54 metres up in a tree in the ancient redwood forest in California, from December 10, 1997, to December 18, 1999. That's 738 days. Straight. Seriously.

"I didn't come from a background of activism," said the 23-year-old woman from Arkansas. But when she was climbing and hiking through the valleys and mountains of the U.S. west coast, she learned that much of the majestic old-growth forests, thousands of years old, were under threat from clearcut logging. "I fell to the ground and started crying," she said, "and immediately got involved."

Julia chose her favourite tree, named it "Luna," and climbed up to perch in its branches — not planning to break any world tree-sitting records, but having simply promised herself that she would not come down without a guarantee that the 1000-year-old tree would survive. She remained focused when lumber workers tried to frighten her down, and

braced herself against the devastating sight of beautiful trees crashing to the ground around her. When security guards swore at her, Julia sang back. When she began to doubt that she could continue, she learned, from watching Luna and the other trees, to stand firm and grounded during storms, yet be willing to bend. Finally, after two long years, a deal was reached with the Pacific Lumber/Maxxam Corporation. Julia had succeeded in saving Luna, along with acres of land surrounding it.

Do I have to spend two years in a tree to make a difference? Of course not! The point of Julia's story — and of this book — is that *anybody* can make a difference. You don't have to be a genius at math or public speaking, or have a history of volunteering since the age of five. Each and every one of us can do *huge* things. Mother Teresa, Nelson Mandela, and Terry Fox, for instance, were all regular people who changed the world in extraordinary ways. But you don't have to be the next Mother Teresa to make a difference. You only have to be you, and make the unique difference that only you can.

Julia is only one among a tide of young people, in every part of the globe, who are working to realize their ideals in concrete ways. They stand firm and grounded during the tough storms, yet are willing to bend and change, to make the world a better place. Since the inception of Free the Children in 1995, we have witnessed many important actions by thousands of youth who have joined the ranks of our worldwide network. For example:

- In Toronto, Canada, young people came together in their efforts to provide emergency relief to children in Afghanistan. They collected over

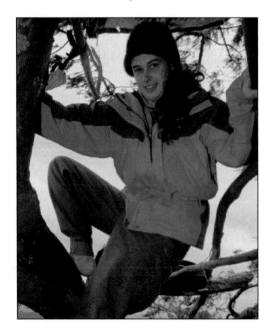

Julia Butterfly Hill braved the intense winds and cold of two harsh winters, suffering from frostbite on her fingers and toes during her sit in the 1000-year-old tree she named Luna.

10 000 school and health kits, and thousands of blankets, winter coats, and toys to deliver to refugees in need.

- In Rio de Janeiro, Brazil, young people launched a campaign that was instrumental in pressuring the government to commit one million dollars toward a nation-wide program to combat exploitative child labour. The group also persuaded dozens of teachers to volunteer their time to teach basic literacy skills to child labourers, and convinced many corporations to donate school and health supplies to rural learning centres.

- In Munich, Germany, young people created the Children Paint Their Dreams initiative, encouraging their peers around the world, particularly those living amid the upheaval of war, to express their fears and dreams in art form. An exhibition of artwork collected by the group has travelled the world, raising awareness of the hardships and the hopes of the world's children.

- In Calcutta, India, youth helped to gather evidence of the trafficking of children to the Middle East for use as drug carriers and to ride racing camels. Presenting their findings before the Indian government and courts, they convinced the President of India to send a representative to Saudi Arabia to negotiate the release of the enslaved children.

These examples are a tiny few compared with the overwhelming number of stories of people who continue to make a difference in their communities and the world. Throughout the continents, young people are seeking ways to promote **solidarity**, or unity — an awareness of how interconnected we are as a human race. This solidarity dissolves the borders between countries, and deepens our understanding of the word "citizenship." Based on the Latin *civitas*, meaning people united in a city or community, the word **citizen** was first used to refer to one who was granted specific rights and responsibilities as a member of a state or nation. More and more, however, we are coming to realize that we are not only members of our nations, but also of our world as a whole.

Welcome to the era of the **global citizen**, of rapidly growing numbers of people — especially youth — turning a critical eye to the evening news, speaking out for justice, coming up with creative ways to address the causes of human suffering, and taking action for the well-being of others. Theirs is a vision of the world as a global community, in which there are no outsiders. It comes from the knowledge that we are all human, and we have only one planet to share, so the problems and struggles and issues that used to be "over there" — other people's hunger, other people's wars — become our own. When one person suffers, we all suffer. When one of us does not survive, a part of us all is lost. When the environment is hurting, we all feel the effects. In other words, we share this world with at least six billion neighbours, and we need to look out for one another.

In this age of the Internet and 24-hour news stations, it is no longer possible to claim ignorance as an excuse for not acting to resolve the inequalities and injustices around us. We are exposed to these realities every day. We have all seen thousands of images of famine, poverty, refugees, environmental destruction, and

> "We have learned that we cannot live alone, at peace; that our own well-being is dependent on the well-being of other nations, far away.... We have learned to be citizens of the world, members of the human community."
>
> — Franklin D. Roosevelt (1882–1945) Former President of the United States

war. But somebody *else* is taking care of those problems, right? Don't we have the United Nations or charities to do something about them? Plus, many young people think, *I'm just a student. I can't vote. And these issues are way too huge—how am I supposed to stop wars? I don't control companies. I'm not the Prime Minister.*

Global citizenship means recognizing that the world's problems are massive and overwhelming, but that you *can* make a difference, and more importantly, you *do*.

You may be thinking, *I had nothing to do with creating these problems. I've just been sitting here, minding my own business, trying to get decent marks or hanging out with my friends. I shouldn't be responsible for solving them.* Keep in mind, however, that the most serious problems our world faces have grown out of the accumulated actions of millions of people, many of whom are simply going about their lives with the best of intentions. Your own daily routine just may play a part. For instance, have you ever:

- Thrown something away when it could have been recycled or composted?

- Bought brand-name clothing from a company with a reputation for exploiting its workers?

- Walked past a homeless person and pretended not to see him or her?

- Told a racist joke?

- Joined in teasing the unpopular kid at school?

- Driven the car to school?

- Used a printer for only one side of a page?

- Rented a violent movie?

- Taken a long shower?

The fact is that small, negative actions like these do add up. The same is true, however, for small, *positive* actions. This brings us to the second key point of this book: The actions you take to make a difference do not have to be huge. They can be easy, meaningful actions that change the world in little ways each day — like smiling at a neighbour or bringing your lunch in a reusable container instead of a plastic bag. Just as Julia Butterfly Hill said, we make a difference every moment, with every action we take. The question is whether our difference is for the better or for the worse.

Let's try that list again. Have you ever:

- Carried a glass bottle all the way home to put into the recycling bin?

- Worn a shirt without any logos or (even better) with a positive message?

- Given a homeless person a cup of coffee or a warm smile?

- Made an effort to be friends with a student of a different culture?

- Stuck up for someone who was being teased?

- Walked or ridden your bike to school?

- Printed on both sides of a page?

- Rented a documentary or a movie with a serious message?

- Turned the shower off as you shampoo to save water?

We are all responsible in some way for the state of our world. Thinking globally leads us to consider how every action we take locally affects our six billion neighbours, and the Earth that we all share. It reveals that our choices are incredibly powerful instruments for effecting change, whether negative or positive. And when more and more people become aware of this power and commit to using it with passion and with purpose, it is the beginning of a healthier world.

A global citizen:

- Takes an interest in global issues, asks questions about established assumptions and practices, and questions the answers provided

- Cares about what he or she believes is right and wrong, just and unjust

- Lives and acts in a way that reflects these beliefs

- Carefully considers every action he or she takes and how it impacts all neighbours around the globe, trying to make choices with positive impacts

- Strives for a more just and sustainable world, and celebrates diversity and solidarity in this mission

This is the essence of **global citizenship**, which makes the difference between living in a world that we just accept, and taking concrete action — small and large — to create the world that we want. This could mean living in a tree for two years, or participating in a canned food drive, or offering a kind word to someone who looks discouraged. It means bringing our actions into line with our values: not merely blaming others and complaining about the problems that we see, but also believing that a better world is possible and working to make it real. It is about discovering that if we want our world to change, the change has to begin with us.

Throughout this book, you will discover a range of issues, problems, stories, ideas, actions, and solutions that

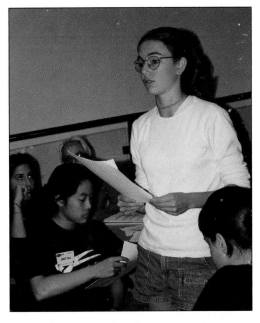

Taking concrete action could mean speaking to others about an issue that is important to you.

will help you to develop your values. **Values** are the beliefs you hold about what is really important, and they guide your choices and behaviour. Your values evolve over the entire course of your lifetime — they come from the general beliefs of your society, and from the personal experiences and thoughts that shape your own unique perspective. We all have values, but being a global citizen means promoting and acting in accordance with your values in seeking a happier, more just society. As you read on, reflect occasionally on what your values are, and how they can contribute to your community, your country, and your world.

The Global Struggle for Human Rights

If global citizenship entails working together for a world that reflects our values, it would make sense for us to agree on some common values that we could all promote and defend. Perhaps the most common value we share as a human race is the "golden rule," which

"Injustice anywhere is a threat to justice everywhere."

— Martin Luther King, Jr. (1929–1968) Civil rights leader

holds that we should treat others as we ourselves would like to be treated. This principle of fairness and mutual respect has been the foundation of global human rights, influencing beliefs, laws, and institutions for centuries. As early as 1215, England's Magna Carta, a charter granted by King John, established rights for all its citizens. In 1776, the Fathers of the American Revolution, led by Thomas Jefferson, declared it a "self-evident" truth that "all men are created equal," and soon followed this with an advanced, ever-evolving Bill of Rights in their Constitution. The early days of the French Revolution led to the Declaration of the Rights of Man and the Citizen in 1789. These legislative landmarks, however, were still exclusive of women, non-whites, and the poor. Never before had the international community declared that every human being had rights — and stated these rights clearly — until the horrors of World War II compelled them to do so.

World War II (1938–1945) was one of the most devastating, deadly wars in history. Millions of people died on the battlefield. Millions of Jews were killed. The Jews, as well as Gypsies, political enemies, people with disabilities, and homosexuals were systematically executed in concentration camps during the Holocaust. A hundred thousand more were wiped out in a matter of minutes by nuclear bombs that fell on Hiroshima and Nagasaki, Japan. At the end of that war, the human race made itself a promise — a promise to its children: Never Again. Never again would we allow our differences to divide us in a way that violated our basic, common values. Never again would we allow such atrocities to be committed against anyone, for any reason.

In 1945 (before the end of World War II), delegates from 50 countries gathered in San Francisco to create the United Nations (UN), with a vision for

INTERNATIONAL LAW AT A GLANCE

Simply put, international law is a set of rules and norms that regulates the conduct of states in the international system or community. Its highest judicial authority is the International Court of Justice, which was established in the United Nations Charter.

International law is derived from two sources: treaties and customary practices, through which states establish rights and responsibilities that govern their relationships with one another.

An international treaty is a source of international law when it is signed and ratified by countries. The treaty becomes legally binding only to those countries that choose to sign and ratify it. "Signed" means that a country says "This sounds good in principle," and "ratified" means "We agree to be legally bound by this treaty." Examples of treaties are the United Nations Charter, the International Covenant on Civil and Political Rights, and the United Nations Convention on the Rights of the Child. In addition to international treaty law, there also exist rules and norms that are the result of long practice among states, and they are known as international customary law.

Because there are rarely any serious repercussions for violating international law, countries that are parties to a treaty sometimes do not live up to their obligations. Until they are willing to commit to truly upholding rights themselves, and find a way to enforce the law, we continue to use international law more as a form of moral expression and pressure. Enforcement mechanisms are within reach, however. The World Trade Organization (WTO) has very strict rules regarding international economics and trade, and it enforces them by imposing financial penalties against countries that violate the rules. Many people hope that some day human rights, the environment, and other social issues will have the same enforceable backing of international law that economics and business have.

international co-operation, peace, and security. In the words of the first article of the UN Charter, signed on June 26, 1945, the new worldwide organization would work toward "promoting and encouraging respect for human rights and for fundamental freedoms for all without distinction as to race, sex, language or religion." This statement meant that every person on Earth was entitled to the rights that enforced his or her dignity and value, but was also responsible for granting these rights to others. It was intended to unite us all in building a more peaceful, equitable, and humane world.

In 1948, the UN General Assembly (the branch of the UN with representatives from every member country) adopted the Universal Declaration of Human Rights to embody the most basic values that we share, and to express with one, united voice, that these rights are not to be violated. This document succeeded in bringing the language and concept of justice, equality, and fundamental freedoms to the attention of the world. However, it has not been successful so far in realizing the ideals it envisioned. Genocides (the systematic

killing of an entire identity group) of millions of people in countries such as Cambodia (1975–1979) and Rwanda (1994) have gone unchecked by the global community. Wars, terrorism, and torture continue to rage uncontrollably throughout the world. Hundreds of thousands of children have no access to clean water or an education. Our promise of "Never Again" has yet to be fulfilled. But it *can* be fulfilled as global citizens commit to taking action to realize the dream of universal human rights. On pages 8 and 9 are a few key articles of the Universal Declaration of Human Rights, and comments on what work remains to be done.

More than fifty years after these rights were recognized, we are still struggling to uphold their ideals. Development experts agree that in order to target violence and conflict at their root, we need to undertake a massive international effort to reduce poverty, illiteracy, and injustice, and to promote democratic principles and human rights. As global citizens, we must make this our mission as we begin to take action within our local, national, and global communities.

"I dream of giving birth to a child who will ask, 'Mother, what was war?'"

— Eve Merriam
(1916–1992)
Author

FROM THE UNIVERSAL DECLARATION OF HUMAN RIGHTS

Article 1: All human beings are born free and equal in dignity and rights.
UN reports indicate that girls and women in many societies are denied their rights to adequate health care, nutrition, and education, in addition to being exposed to sexual abuse, genital mutilation, and forced marriage. Around the world, individuals are denied basic needs and freedoms, and are exposed to violence and exploitation simply because of their skin colour, ethnic background, religion, or other identity group.

Article 3: Everyone has the right to life, liberty and security of person.
According to the UN High Commissioner for Refugees, there are nearly 20 million displaced persons or refugees from 160 countries in the world today, forced to flee their homes because of armed conflict or natural disasters, and pushed into unstable conditions, without shelter or land to grow food. In many countries, political opponents or members of targeted groups are routinely jailed without trial, tortured, or killed.

Article 4: No one shall be held in slavery or servitude.
The UN Office on Drugs and Crime reports that more than 700 000 men, women, and children are trafficked every year for the purposes of bonded and forced labour in factories, agriculture, or domestic servitude. Many of these workers are also physically confined, threatened with violence, and sexually exploited.

Article 5: No one shall be subjected to torture or to cruel, inhuman or degrading treatment or punishment.
According to the International Rehabilitation Council for Torture Victims, torture continues to be practised regularly in up to 100 countries. Individuals who speak out against torture in their own countries are often subject to repression and harassment, and are even tortured themselves.

Article 7: All are equal before the law and are entitled without discrimination to equal protection of the law.
Although more white people commit drug offences than do African Americans in the United States, black people constitute 62.7% of all drug offenders sent to state prisons, and black men are sent to prison on drug charges at 13.4 times the rate of white men, according to Human Rights Watch. The Native Women's Association of Canada reports that although Aboriginal women represent only 2% of Canada's population, they make up 27% of all women serving federal jail time (sentences of 2 years or more).

"How lovely to think that no one need wait a moment, we can start now, start slowly changing the world!"

— Anne Frank (1929–1945) Diarist, Holocaust victim

Article 20: Everyone has the right to freedom of peaceful assembly and association.

Human Rights Watch reports that in the 1990s, over 20 000 American workers each year suffered reprisals for exercising their right to freedom of association. Millions of workers in the United States, including farm workers, domestic workers and immigrant workers, do not have collective bargaining rights under any law, and thus cannot negotiate with their employers to determine wages, hours, rules and working conditions. In many countries, unions are illegal and union leaders are jailed for their activities.

Article 21: Everyone has the right to take part in the government of his/her country, directly or through freely chosen representatives.

According to the International Institute for Democracy and Electoral Assistance, women, who make up over 52% of the world's population, held only 14% of legislative seats worldwide in 2002. Billions of people live under dictatorships, one-party governments, or corrupt democracies. They are either denied the vote or their votes are virtually ignored. In such countries, political candidates are frequently threatened, jailed, or killed during elections.

Article 23: Everyone has the right to work, to free choice of employment, to just and favourable conditions of work and to protection against unemployment.

The International Labour Organization estimates that one billion women and men are currently unemployed, underemployed, or are "working poor." National labour standards are non-existent or ignored in thousands of free-trade zones around the world (areas in which commerce is unrestricted by duties or tariff regulations). This can lead to extremely exploitative labour conditions in which workers are not paid a living wage and are exposed to severe health hazards and physical abuse by their employers.

Article 26: Everyone has the right to education.

UNICEF reports that over 130 million children of primary school age in developing countries, including 73 million girls, are growing up without access to basic education. Where there are schools, there are often no teachers, desks, or supplies to learn in a productive environment. UNESCO (United Nations Educational, Scientific and Cultural Organization) estimates that there are 862 million illiterate adults in the world, two thirds of whom are women.

> *"We will spare no effort to free our fellow men, women, and children from the abject and dehumanizing conditions of extreme poverty, to which more than a billion of them are currently subjected."*
>
> — United Nations Millennium Declaration (September 2000)

Human Rights in Canada

Because the Universal Declaration of Human Rights is more a statement of ideals than an effective guarantee of our fundamental rights and freedoms, we rely on our individual countries to protect our human rights. Canadians are among the best-protected people in the world because our rights and freedoms are guaranteed under our Constitution. Canada's human rights record is a tremendous accomplishment for our society, and a source of pride for our citizens. However, overcoming racism, discrimination, and inequality has not always been easy, and the struggle continues today.

> "There's no question in my mind but that rights are never won unless people are willing to fight for them."
>
> — Eleanor Smeal (b. 1930) Women's rights leader

HUMAN RIGHTS EVENTS IN CANADA

1885: A discriminatory $50 head tax is placed on immigrants from China. The tax is later raised to $500 in 1903, before a complete ban on immigration from China is imposed from 1923 to 1947.

1916: Women are granted the right to vote and run in provincial elections in Manitoba. The federal government follows suit in 1918, and Québec is the final province to do so in 1940. Women cannot be appointed to the Senate until the 1929 Persons Case.

1947: Canadians of Asian descent are granted the right to vote and run in federal elections. First Nations peoples have to wait until 1960.

1947: Saskatchewan is the first province to enact a Bill of Rights, prohibiting discrimination on the basis of race, religion, colour, and national origin, as well as proclaiming freedoms of assembly and association.

1952: Blacks and Asians, as well as people with epilepsy, people with mental and physical disabilities, and homosexuals are restricted from immigrating to Canada. It is not until 1976 that discrimination is finally prohibited in immigration policy.

1960: Prime Minister John Diefenbaker passes the Canadian Bill of Rights. For the first time, *all* Canadians are guaranteed specified rights and freedoms in law. The Bill of Rights, though, applies only to federal laws, and because it is not entrenched in the Constitution, it does not have the power to automatically overrule other federal laws.

1977: The Canadian Human Rights Act is passed, prohibiting discrimination in federal employment and services.

1982: Prime Minister Pierre Trudeau leads the repatriation of the Canadian Constitution, including an enshrined Charter of Rights and Freedoms.

The Charter of Rights and Freedoms is generally acknowledged as one of the greatest social and political achievements in Canadian history. By being entrenched in the newly repatriated Canadian Constitution, its provisions supersede *all* federal and provincial legislation and policies. It truly guarantees our fundamental rights and freedoms, and it gives the judicial system the power to declare a law or policy unconstitutional, and therefore invalid, if it violates the Charter. Some of the major articles of the Charter include:

Section 2: Everyone has the following fundamental freedoms
a) freedom of conscience and religion;
b) freedom of thought, belief, opinion and expression …;
c) freedom of peaceful assembly; and
d) freedom of association.

Section 3: Every citizen of Canada has the right to vote … .

Section 6 (2): Every citizen of Canada … has the right
a) to move to and take up residence in any province; and
b) to pursue the gaining of a livelihood in any province.

Section 7: Everyone has the right to life, liberty and security of the person … .

Section 9: Everyone has the right not to be arbitrarily detained or imprisoned.

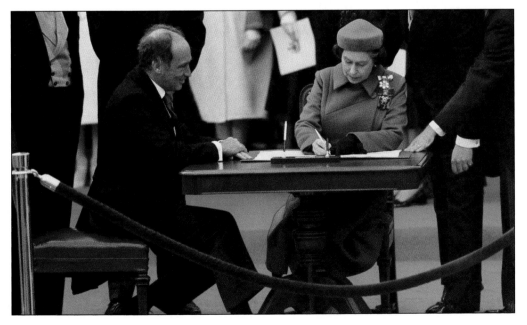

Prime Minister Trudeau watches as Queen Elizabeth II signs the Constitution into law on April 17, 1982, on Parliament Hill.

Section 15 (1): Every individual is equal before and under the law and has the right to the equal protection and equal benefit of the law without discrimination and, in particular, without discrimination based on race, national or ethnic origin, colour, religion, sex, age or mental or physical disability.

The Charter puts two limits on the rights and freedoms within it. First, in Section 1, it declares that the rights and freedoms are "subject only to such reasonable limits prescribed by law as can be demonstrably justified in a free and democratic society." In other words, if it can be shown that a law violating any right or freedom is justified, that law is valid. Such a case happened in *Canada (Human Rights Comm.) v. Taylor* (1990), when the Supreme Court of Canada ruled that restricting hate propaganda is a reasonable limit on the freedom of expression. The second limit on the rights and freedoms in the Charter is included in Section 33: the "notwithstanding clause" that allows provincial or federal legislatures to overrule the Charter. This clause is only meant to be used in extreme circumstances, and such a law must be renewed every five years.

PROMINENT HUMAN RIGHTS ACTIVISTS IN CANADA

The protection of human rights is not automatic — it requires the vigilance, passion, and action of all citizens. Within our borders and beyond, there are millions of people whose rights are threatened or non-existent, and around the world, many individual Canadians dedicate their lives to the struggle for human rights. Here are some of these activists.

Louise Arbour

Louise Arbour led a highly publicized Commission of Inquiry into conditions at the Kingston Prison for Women in 1995, before becoming a world-renowned legal advocate for human rights. In 1996, she was appointed Chief War Crimes Prosecutor for the International War Crimes Tribunal in The Hague, where she prosecuted those involved in crimes against humanity in Rwanda and the former Yugoslavia. In 1999, Justice Arbour was appointed to the Supreme Court of Canada. In 2004, she was named United Nations High Commissioner for Human Rights.

Matthew Coon Come

Matthew Coon Come was the Chief of the Cree Nation when he stood resolutely opposed to the Québec Referendum on secession from Canada in 1995, and held his own referendum, which voted 96% "no" to the Cree (and their 400 000 square kilometres) leaving Canada. As National Chief of the Assembly of First Nations from 2000–2003, he spoke out against the practices of individual tribal leaders, brought the plight of Canada's Aboriginal peoples into the international spotlight at the United Nations, and forcefully opposed the federal government's First Nations Governing Act because it did not go far enough to grant the right of self-governance to his people.

Take Action!

1 Examine the full United Nations Universal Declaration of Human Rights. Which rights do you value the most? Why? Are there rights you value that are not included in the document? Discuss these rights with a partner.

2 Select one of the human rights listed in the Universal Declaration, and research the world's progress on making that right a reality. Answer the following questions:

   • In which countries is that right being violated?

   • How is it being violated, and how many people are affected?

   • What efforts have been made to enforce that right?

   • What organizations are working to report violations and advocate for better enforcement?

3 Write a letter to your federal Member of Parliament to express your concern about the human right you researched above. Ask what the Government of Canada has done and can do to ensure better enforcement. See the Plugging Into the Political System section (page 113) for more details.

With Rights Come Great Responsibilities

Being a citizen of any society, including the global society, is an interdependent relationship. Along with the right to enjoy Earth's resources, and the freedoms promised to us in the Universal Declaration of Human Rights, comes a fundamental responsibility to treat the world and its inhabitants with respect, and to actively work to create the future that we want to see. As Article 29 of the Universal Declaration states, "everyone has duties to the community in which alone the free and full development of his personality is possible."

In addition to being global citizens, we are also fortunate citizens of an amazing country — Canada. Our democratic social system is built upon the values of equality, respect, freedom, peace, and rule of law. These values come together to protect us from harm and help us fulfill our life goals. In exchange for our contribution to society, Canadians are guaranteed many specific rights in the Constitution's Charter of Rights and Freedoms. Can you imagine what would happen if no one contributed by fulfilling his or her social responsibilities? Our society would simply not be capable of providing those cherished freedoms. If no one voted, we would have no government. If no one respected the law, no one would be safe. If no one paid taxes, we would have no schools, no hospitals, no roads, no garbage pickup, or fire department, among other things.

Not having the vote does not excuse young people from their responsibilities to society. Civic participation in a democracy should happen a lot more often than once every four or five years! Remember, compared with citizens of many other countries around the world, Canadians have many important rights and liberties. This also means greater responsibilities.

Citizenship, in essence, is social responsibility *in action*. A healthy democracy depends on the participation of concerned and informed citizens who work to build a society that reflects their values. This means having a vision of a more just world, and taking action

Canadian Rights and Responsibilities

Rights	Responsibilities
Legal rights: right to life, liberty, and security of person	Obeying Canada's laws
Equality rights: right to protection against discrimination, equality under law	Standing up to discrimination and injustice; celebrating cultural and other differences
Democratic rights: the right to run and vote in an election	Voting in elections; researching and discussing the issues at election time; supporting the campaign of a local candidate
Freedom of thought, expression, religion, belief, opinion	Expressing opinions on issues that you care about freely and passionately while respecting the opinions, rights, and freedoms of others
Mobility rights: right to live and work anywhere in Canada	Caring for, appreciating, and protecting our beautiful environment, coast to coast to coast
The right to peaceful assembly	Active participation in your community, especially volunteering, helping, and getting to know other people

to bring it into reality. Remember, the rights that we have today were not given — they were won after years of long, difficult struggle against unfair attitudes and laws. For example, would you believe that, despite being granted the right to vote in 1918, Canadian women were not considered "persons"? Because only "persons" were eligible to be appointed to government offices, such as the Senate, that privilege was strictly reserved for men. Outraged, five women from Alberta launched a campaign to have women legally recognized as persons, and refused to give up, no matter how fiercely they were criticized. The courage and determination of the "Famous Five" succeeded in 1929, ending the exclusion of women from the Senate and creating a more just Canadian society. Where would we be if these women had not taken a stand?

Today, it seems impossible to imagine a Canada in which women are not considered "persons." But imagine the world fifty years from now. What will future generations think of our society? What rights are we still lacking today that you feel should be recognized in the future? Throughout this book, you will find countless issues, ideas, and skills to help you create your vision of an ideal world, and start working toward it as an inspired Canadian and global citizen.

Nellie McClung, one of Alberta's "Famous Five," campaigned ceaselessly to improve the rights of Canadian women.

> "It is so much easier sometimes to sit down and be resigned than to rise up and be indignant."
>
> — Nellie McClung (1873–1951) Suffragist, politician

Take Action!

1 Brainstorm all the ways you have fulfilled your responsibilities as a Canadian citizen today, this week, and this year. Come up with three more ways that you can add to your list starting today. Repeat the brainstorm, thinking as a global citizen on global issues such as human rights and the environment.

2 Picture your ideal world. What component of your picture is missing in today's society? Why is it missing? What can *you* do to make that dream a reality? List two concrete actions that you can take to begin advocating for the future you want to see.

3 Meet up with some friends from different cultural backgrounds, and ask them what global citizenship means to them. What rights and responsibilities are most important to them? How do their lists differ from yours? How are they the same?

The Leader in YOUth

You do *not* have to wait to start making a positive difference in the world. You do not have to put it off until you pull up your grades or are old enough to vote, drive, graduate from high school, or get a part-time job. You do *not* have to be perfect to change the world. You only have to be willing to change, to try to make a difference, and encourage the people around you to do the same. The world needs you now, just as you are. As a young person. The time for letting adults do all the work to build the world that *we* are going to inherit has long passed. We are not called upon only to be the leaders of tomorrow; we must also be the leaders of today!

Within this book, you will find a number of examples of youth, just like you, who one day decided that something had to be done about a problem and that they were ready to take on the challenge. You will meet Cheryl Perera, who travelled to Sri Lanka to document the rise of child labour in that country; and Jean-Dominic Lévesque-René, who fought to ban the use of pesticides in Québec after discovering their link to his own cancer. You will also learn about Dalal Al-Waheidi, who grew up amid war and uncertainty in the Middle East, and remains devoted to promoting a culture of peace and dialogue.

Young people have the power to be "a beacon of freedom, a beacon of justice, and a beacon of light to the world," declared Hafsat Abiola, a young human rights activist from Nigeria. Committed to the empowerment of women and youth, Hafsat founded an organization called the Kudirat Initiative for Democracy (KIND), named for her mother, to continue the legacy of her parents, whose courageous struggle for freedom and justice in Nigeria led to their assassination. Speaking to her young peers at an international assembly in San Francisco, she urged them to use their "inner light to do amazingly beautiful work …. If this connects with others, the internal light will become external, and you can set our whole planet aglow."

IDENTIFYING YOUR GIFTS

Everyone has something unique to contribute to the world, even though we sometimes don't have the confidence to admit it. Think about what you love to do, or what interests you. Whether it's sports, or art, or hanging out with friends, what lights you up is often where you'll find your gift, because it brings out the best in you. We are all gifted in some way, but not in every way — so we have to share our talents to help one another, to lift one another up. Ask yourself: *What are my gifts and talents, and how can I use them to make a difference in the world?* See the chart on the following page to give you some ideas.

When we all put our gifts and talents together, we become a team of world-changing, difference-making, global citizens. Seek out others with gifts that are different from yours, and discover how powerful you can be as a team!

Gift		Service
Good listener	→	Join a peer-counselling group; be known among your friends as the one who is always there to help them through difficult times.
Physical strength	→	Shovel your elderly neighbour's driveway; stick up for the students getting bullied at school (without violence, of course!).
Bilingual	→	Tutor other students in one of your languages; help new immigrants who speak that language to adjust and get settled.
Good writer	→	Start a school newspaper devoted to social issues; draft letters to Members of Parliament for a social cause.
Good speaker	→	Run for student council and create positive change; speak at your school or a place of worship about an issue that concerns you.
Outgoing	→	Reach out to welcome new students; be the spokesperson for a social action group at school; recruit new members.
Athletic	→	Organize a sports tournament to raise awareness and funds for charity.
Musical	→	Organize a charity concert or open-mike night at school with the participation of local bands; write a song about an issue, or put together a whole CD!
Artistic	→	Start a community mural project that invites participants to express their thoughts about an issue in a group painting; design greeting cards to sell during the holidays as a fundraiser for charity.

"There is a vitality, a life force, an energy, a quickening, that is translated through you into action.

And because there is only one you in all time, this expression is unique.

If you block it, it will never exist through any other medium and will be lost.

The world will not have it.

It is not your business to determine how good it is, nor how it compares with other expression.

It is your business to keep the channel open."

— Martha Graham (1894–1991) Dancer, choreographer, and teacher

CRAIG KIELBURGER: REDEFINING "GIFTED"

I was doing a CBC interview, a few years ago, for a television show that was taking a look at youth who had accomplished a great deal very early in their lives. One other guy was being interviewed with me. He was 19, had already completed his Masters degree and PhD and was working at a pharmaceutical company. He told the host and myself on air that he was "gifted." He had discovered this fact in Grade Three, when he passed a special IQ test that determines how gifted or average you are.

Several times throughout the conversation, this guy explained his many accomplishments in terms of being "gifted." He must have said the word "gifted" at least five times during the interview. Finally, the host turned to me and asked, "Are you gifted, Craig?" I looked at her, and then at him, and shook my head, "no."

Later that day, I was still thinking about the interview when I went back to the Free the Children office. As I looked around at the remarkable young people who work with us, I realized that I had given the host the wrong answer. I saw our Web master, whom we all consider to be incredibly gifted when it comes to designing Web sites that are visited by millions of people around the world. I saw our young writing staff, who are so talented at translating our passion and energy into words that inspire others to become involved. I saw our wonderful student volunteers who are gifted at organizing, raising funds, and communicating with others. I thought of all of the young people I know who are gifted in art, or music or sports, or who are compassionate listeners, terrific in business matters, or at making others laugh. As a matter of fact, I couldn't think of a single person I knew who wasn't gifted. I realized that each one of us is born with special gifts or talents, but no single person is gifted in all ways. We are all pieces of a complex puzzle, a mosaic. And only by sharing our special gifts or talents can we complete it, and create a happier and more fulfilling world.

> *"What lies behind us and what lies before us are tiny matters compared to what lies within us."*
>
> — Ralph Waldo Emerson
> (1803–1882)
> Lecturer, poet,
> and essayist

Take Action!

1 Finish these sentences: "People always tell me that I am good at _____!" and "In my spare time, I love to _____." Next, write down as many of your gifts, skills, and strengths as you can (aim for at least ten). Come up with a way that you can use each one to help make a difference in your community.

2 Choose one particularly useful gift from your list, and offer it to a school club or social justice organization. If they do not need the kind of help you are offering right now, find an organization that can use your gifts to their fullest.

3 Dream big now! Envision a way for you to use your most potent gift full time, for the rest of your life. Identify a career that would allow you to use your unique gift for the betterment of the world. Describe your "dream job" in 250 to 300 words.

PROFILE Nadja Halilbegovich: A Global Citizen

When Nadja Halilbegovich was 12, her vision of the world changed forever. In 1992, the violent regional conflict in the former Yugoslavia spread to Sarajevo, the capital of Bosnia, Nadja's beautiful homeland. Sarajevo became a city plagued with danger and death, where the sounds of sirens and grenades were constant. Nadja was injured when a bombshell exploded close to her home, and her family was forced to take shelter for months at a time in the basement of their apartment building. Although physically trapped and wounded, Nadja was determined to free and nourish her mind and soul.

By recording her thoughts in a diary, Nadja maintained the courage to dream of escaping the fighting and hatred, of the things she wanted to do, and the person she wanted to become. But the daily realities of war tested her strength. Nadja drew from the courage of her parents, and fought against words of pessimism and misery by replacing them with poems of hope and peace. Nadja used her artistic talents to inspire her fellow Bosnians to keep their hope alive. She read excerpts of her diary entries and poetry on national radio, and shared her music with her choir in schools, hospitals, and at religious gatherings. When Nadja was 14, as the war raged on, her diary was published as *Sarajevo Childhood Wounded by War*. It was proof that, even in the worst of conditions, dreams could come true.

Today, Nadja lives in Canada with the lessons that she gained through the war. Surviving the conflict has made her grateful, not bitter, and committed to achieving a peaceful future. She is an activist against injustice and intolerance, speaking out for the children of Bosnia who did not survive. In 2002, as a member of Free the Children's Embracing Cultures Project, she travelled to more than 150 schools across North America to share her experience of the war as an example of what can happen when differences between human beings are not valued and respected, and how crucial it is to move beyond merely *tolerating* other cultures to actively and wholeheartedly *embracing* them.

1 What attributes of a global citizen do you find in Nadja?
2 Which of these attributes do you possess? Which would you like to develop?
3 Is having hope essential to being a global citizen? Write out a statement that will inspire you to maintain your hope for a better world, even when you face a difficult issue.

2

Becoming Global Citizens: A Question of Choice

CONTENTS

To Act or Not to Act

In 1995, Canadian General Roméo Dallaire was leading the United Nations peacekeeping force in Rwanda, a country in East Africa. He was desperately troubled by evidence that something terrible was about to happen. Ethnic hatred between ancient tribal groups was boiling over, fuelled by the struggle for political power: members of the Hutu majority were planning a massive, merciless attack on the Tutsi minority. Dallaire communicated with the United Nations Security Council, made up of the five most powerful countries (the United States, the United Kingdom, France, Russia, and China) and ten others. He repeatedly stressed that immediate action had to be taken to avert an all-out genocide, with deaths expected in the millions. More troops were needed, and they required the authorization to take all necessary action to stop the impending devastation.

The Security Council forced Dallaire to back down. Ten Belgian soldiers from Dallaire's unit were killed, and the entire UN force was removed from Rwanda. In the following months, an estimated 800 000 Tutsis were massacred, raped, beaten, chopped up with machetes, and buried in mass graves. It was exactly as Dallaire had forewarned. The world stood by and did nothing.

General Dallaire has since spoken out powerfully against the inaction of the United Nations, especially the members of the Security Council. The Rwandan genocide was preventable, he said, and so were many others that have happened since the famous "Never Again" promise following the Holocaust and World War II.

A UNICEF official declared General Roméo Dallaire (left) "the one shining beacon" during the tragedy in Rwanda.

The sheer size of global problems like these often makes us feel powerless, useless, helpless — that's why most people do not help. It is important to understand, however, that major struggles often start out as small issues. Conflicts escalate into wars when individuals stand by and do nothing. The Hutu and Tutsi once lived as neighbours and as friends. Individuals in their communities failed to take a stand when violence against neighbours began; the international community failed to take a stand when the massacres occurred. We are always told that our actions have consequences, but *inaction* has consequences too. When we stay silent or look the other way, we are bystanders to a problem, and we contribute to making it worse.

Jody Williams, who won the Nobel Peace Prize in 1997 for her leadership in the struggle to ban landmines, once said, "compassion without action is meaningless." In our own lives, we are challenged on a daily basis to take a stand for the rights of others.

> "First they came for the Jews, and I did not speak out, because I was not a Jew.
> Then they came for the Communists, and I did not speak out, because I was not a Communist.
> Then they came for the trade unionists, and I did not speak out, because I was not a trade unionist.
> Then they came for me, and there was no one left, to speak out for me."
>
> — Pastor Martin Niemöller (1892–1984) Lutheran pastor, former president of the World Council of Churches

- Have you ever seen someone being bullied at school?

- Have you ever disagreed with something that your government was doing?

- Have you ever found out that the maker of your favourite food, or your favourite store or company exploits people or pollutes the environment?

- Have you ever seen someone wrongly accused or punished in class?

- Have you ever seen an image of a malnourished child on television?

Each of these scenarios is an opportunity to act. Instead of closing our eyes, walking away, or asking, "Where's the TV remote?" we can ask ourselves, "What can I do?" In many cases, we fail to help not because we do not care, but because we do not understand what should be done, we are afraid to get involved too deeply, or we don't believe that we have what it takes to do anything useful to help. We can easily forget our own guilt when we notice that no one else is helping either, but when everyone assumes that someone else will take charge, no one does anything.

What if the world were made up of only bystanders? What if there were no leaders to take up the challenges that the rest of us choose to shy away from? Slavery would still be legal. No woman, Chinese person, or First Nations person would have the right to vote in Canada. Black South Africans would still be cruelly oppressed under apartheid. As young people, we have far greater power than we think we do. This is our world to build in the image that we want to see. There is no more time to wait around for a superhero to drop from the sky. *We* have the gifts. *We* have the skills. *We* have a heartbeat. It's time to choose. Whom are *you* waiting for?

A Question of Character

It is often said that "character" is who you are when no one is watching. It is what you do when there are no expectations of you, no incentives, and no rewards. It is the choices you make when you are free to do whatever you want, without consequence or judgment. From this perspective, character is how your actions correspond with your values when it matters to no one else — how tall you stand when you alone are in the room. This aspect of character is called "integrity."

Maintaining integrity in the face of a challenge often requires courage. When injustice, wrongdoing, or need stare you in the face, do you flinch or take it on? One of the most famous images of the twentieth century is that of a lone figure standing defiantly in front of a massive advancing tank in China's Tiananmen Square in June 1989. A pro-democracy uprising had prompted the Chinese Army to clear the square, and hundreds of unarmed civilians, including children and elderly people, were shot dead by troops firing into the crowd. Standing before the tank, the young man refused to back down from the ideals he had come there to defend. As the tank moved to avoid him, he kept in front of it, challenging the troops to run him down. Finally, the tank just stopped. For its integrity and courage, his extraordinary act will never be forgotten.

Courage means having the inner strength to do what is right or necessary in spite of fear.

To help us better understand the concept of character as a combination of integrity and courage, we turn to Mahatma Gandhi (1869–1948), a leader in the movement to free India from British rule, and one of the most famous advocates of non-violent action to achieve social change. His two most famous quotations reflect the two key components of character: "I live my message" and "You must be the change you wish to see in the world."

ON INTEGRITY: LIVING YOUR MESSAGE

Can you imagine what people would have thought if Martin Luther King, Jr. had gone home after his celebrated *I Have a Dream* speech and had a fistfight with a white neighbour? What if Anthony Robbins (an American motivational speaker who tells millions of people they can be successful if they try) turned down the opportunity to give an important workshop because he thought he would be a failure? As leaders and global citizens, when we speak up for an issue we care about, people listen. But they also watch us very closely to make sure we practise what we preach. When we violate our own message through our actions, our leadership is called into question, both by those who support us *and* those who oppose us. They call us hypocrites and say, "You have no integrity." They would be right. Consider how you would evaluate the character of someone who:

- Runs a peer group about substance abuse, but gets drunk every weekend

- Warns his or her children never to smoke, but goes through a pack of cigarettes a day

- Demonstrates at peace rallies, but settles a heated argument after school with a fistfight

- Directs a campaign against stereotypes and discrimination, but tells blonde jokes

- Complains about global warming, but drives to school every day instead of biking or taking public transit or the school bus

> "Don't tell me what you believe. Tell me what you do, and then I'll tell you what you believe."
>
> — Stokely Carmichael (1941–1998) Social activist

Even the greatest leaders have found themselves compromising their integrity at times; they are human and imperfect, just as we are. Leadership means *striving* to bring your actions into line with your values, and challenging others to do the same in order to improve not only your society, but also yourselves. For example, Gandhi's struggle for Indian independence involved not only opposition to British colonialism, but also to the Indian caste system (a deep-rooted and discriminatory social hierarchy). He challenged Indians to recognize that, just as the British could no longer oppress them, they could no longer oppress their own. For Gandhi, and those who joined him, the simultaneous development of the moral person and the moral society was key.

It may be difficult to change your own attitudes and habits once you take on a social issue. If you are against war and violence, can you stop playing violent video games or watching violent movies? If you are against unfair trade for farmers in Africa, can you switch from eating your favourite chocolate bar to one sold under fair trade practices? The good news is that when you make a sacrifice that people know is very hard for you, they are more likely to be inspired to follow your example and make similar sacrifices in their own lives. When, as leaders, we are conscious of our own behaviour, others are able to understand our values and aspire to our example. To maximize your effectiveness and your impact as a leader, it is crucial that you not only believe in and deliver your message. You must also, truly, *live your message*.

ON COURAGE: BEING THE CHANGE

Have you ever looked back at a situation and thought, *I really should have had the courage to do something about that*? The character of a global citizen is determined in part by making choices that require courage — to lead by example and to stand up for a better world when no one else will. As the leader of the pro-democracy movement in Burma (now called Myanmar) since the brutal repression of a 1988 uprising, Aung San Suu Kyi was placed under house arrest for six years, unable to see her family, and restricted in her freedom to travel and speak even after her release. Yet she continued her struggle and has drawn international attention to the plight of her nation.

For his determined efforts in the movement against apartheid in South Africa, Nelson Mandela was sentenced to life in prison in 1962, and remained there for 27 years. Before entering confinement, he declared to the world:

I have cherished the ideal of a democratic and free society in which all persons live together in harmony and with equal opportunities. It is an ideal which I hope to live for and achieve. But if need be, it is an ideal for which I am prepared to die.

Wait a minute, you may be thinking. *When I started reading this book I didn't sign up for that kind of commitment*. Well, creating change is not easy. The **status quo**, or the existing state of affairs, is deeply ingrained in social attitudes and practices. It is also perpetuated because it serves the interests of powerful people. Many sacrifices have been made before our time to create the amazing society in which we live. The least we can do to honour those who have struggled in the past is to continue to work toward a better world. Have the courage to not simply talk about the changes you want, but also to *be the change*.

We choose our own battles, and there are few issues that require us to sacrifice our personal health or safety. Just breaking with accepted social norms requires significant doses of courage, especially around friends and family or others who do not understand, and who may mock, disrespect, or ostracize us. Courage at the high school level could mean putting your "cool" factor on the line by befriending a bullied student or speaking out against an offensive joke.

Standing up for what you value is not an easy task, but a very rewarding one. There is an old saying that if you can find a path with no obstacles, it probably doesn't lead anywhere. Think about the heroes you admire, throughout history, in the movies, and in real life. All of them had the courage to take a stand. We tend to look at the negative consequences of standing out from the crowd, but we should focus instead on another crucial point: Courage is something that people respect, and it can inspire them to stand up alongside you. In the end, your character is on display with every action you take, whether people are watching or not. You have to look at yourself in the mirror at the end of every day and be proud of who you are and the choices you make.

> *"The love of our neighbor in all its fullness simply means being able to say to him, 'What are you going through?'"*
>
> — Simone Weil
> (1909–1943)
> Philosopher, mystic, and author

SHARING THE SPOTLIGHT

You've probably heard of these stars, but did you know that they have been working hard to turn the spotlight onto important social issues? More and more, world celebrities are using their fame to spread positive messages and rally people to action. Take a look at what they have been up to, behind and in front of the scenes.

Bono

Lead singer of the band U2, Bono is a vocal social activist who has rallied numerous actors and artists to his causes. As spokesman for the Jubilee 2000 Debt Relief Campaign, now called Drop the Debt, he advocates for a major initiative that would wipe out the $90 billion debt owed by the world's poorest nations to the richest nations, and promote trade reform and a commitment from pharmaceutical companies to provide free HIV drugs to African countries.

Mira Nair

Indian director Mira Nair won an Academy Award nomination for her film *Salaam, Bombay!*, which profiles the lives of street children in Mumbai (Bombay). Her many thought-provoking films have shed light on the struggles of marginalized groups, addressing such issues as the plight of prostitutes in Mumbai, racial tensions between the

African-American and Indian-American communities in the American South, and the experience of Cuban refugees in the United States.

Sarah Polley

Sarah Polley, the Canadian actress who starred in CBC's *Road to Avonlea* and the film *The Sweet Hereafter*, among many other films and television productions, is also a vocal political activist, committed to securing greater public funding for the arts, health care, and welfare. She frequently participates in peaceful protests, including those denouncing the negative effects of globalization. Sarah is working to merge her passions for film and activism by acting in, writing, and directing films with social and political messages.

Oprah Winfrey

Oprah Winfrey has founded numerous charities, including Oprah's Angel Network, a charity that raises money from viewer and celebrity donations. The funds have been put toward granting scholarships for minority students, building homes for Habitat for Humanity, and constructing 34 schools in 10 countries with Free the Children. In 2005, she will open the Oprah Winfrey Leadership Academy for Girls, an education program in South Africa.

Many more public figures, such as Richard Gere, Angelina Jolie, Danny Glover, Susan Sarandon, Dikembe Mutombo, Vince Carter, and Michael Moore, are using their fame to draw attention to urgent social issues. Research celebrities whom you admire for their talent, and find out how they are using it to make a difference!

Take Action!

1 Think of one prominent world leader or a leader in your community whose character you admire. What actions have they taken to reveal their character? Which of their character traits would you most like to develop yourself?

2 Describe a time when you demonstrated global character (as in making a difference in the world), either when no one was watching or when everyone was watching. How did you feel making that choice? How do you feel now, looking back?

3 Brainstorm ways you can improve your integrity — in what ways do you not always live your values or your message? Brainstorm courageous actions to make a difference at school or in your community — what would be the consequences of putting yourself on the line? What would be the consequences of *not* acting? Commit to act on one item from each list and *go for it*.

Ethical Decision Making

Doing the right thing is not always easy. Right and wrong are not always clear-cut, and most situations do not allow us the time to sit down and debate the fine line. While making an **ethical** decision is not always a simple matter, it is always a crucial one, because what we say and do determines not only the shape of our own lives, but also the lives of others. "Ethical," "moral," and "principled" are all various ways of saying "according to your values." They provide us with a general code of conduct that we can follow to keep our actions true to our values. But we cannot always just plug our values into a specific situation and get a printout of the right answer. This section will offer some helpful guidelines and tools that you can use to chart your way through the sea of ethical dilemmas that life throws us.

THE CARE MODEL OF GLOBAL CITIZENSHIP

Although perceptions of right and wrong sometimes differ among people, generations, cultures, and ways of life, a number of values do seem to resonate across social divisions and national borders. Created by a diverse group of people at Leaders Today, the CARE Model of Global Citizenship represents a set of core values that united them all, despite the many differences that existed among them. They are the values at the core of global citizenship, and they have very little to do with the diverse groups to which we belong, and everything to do with our common humanity.

Using the CARE model as a guide to your actions, you can enhance your effectiveness as an active participant in

Compassion
Action
Responsibility
Equality

the world. As you continue to develop your skills as a leader and a global citizen, revisit this model occasionally to make sure that the actions you take reflect your values. This list is by no means exhaustive, and we encourage you to add to or subtract from it as you think about your own values and the things that matter most to you.

Compassion

Have *empathy* for everyone involved: Try to see a situation from all perspectives and to truly understand and take into account the feelings, needs, and motives of others in making your decisions, even when you do not agree with them personally. Show *caring* by being attentive to people's various needs, especially emotional needs, and by treating everyone with kindness, concern, and generosity, regardless of outcomes.

Action

Take *initiative* to act, showing that you are ready to do what it takes to reach a solution. Have *courage* and the strength of mind to control fear and act firmly in the face of difficulties, to do the right thing even when it may be unpopular, and to resist peer pressure to fall in line with accepted but questionable practices. Display *perseverance* in reaching for your goals: Never give up or lose focus on what you have set out to do. Be a shameless *optimist*, seeing beauty, hope, and opportunity in any given situation. Dream big and unapologetically.

Responsibility

Be *trustworthy* and reliable; be *accountable* for all your actions and only make commitments that you can and will honour. Above all, be *honest* — honesty breaks down barriers and allows for finding true, sustainable solutions. Display your *integrity* — be sincere and back it up by living your message. *Help.* When in doubt, seek opportunities that allow you to contribute and give of yourself to someone in need.

Equality

Strive for *fairness* by being sensitive to the needs of each individual, seeking solutions that leave everyone better off. Show *respect* so that others can see it; treat all people with honour, courtesy, dignity, civility, and esteem. Do not just *accept* personal and cultural differences — *celebrate* them. Listen to what others have to say, and be open to the fact that you can learn from them. Always be prepared to agree to disagree in order to salvage a relationship. You will always be better off when you consider your personal relationships to be more important than being right.

PUTTING CARE INTO ACTION

Sometimes we focus so much on upholding one ethical principle that we end up compromising another principle. For example, we might persevere so much in an effort to get a job done that we fail to be compassionate with our

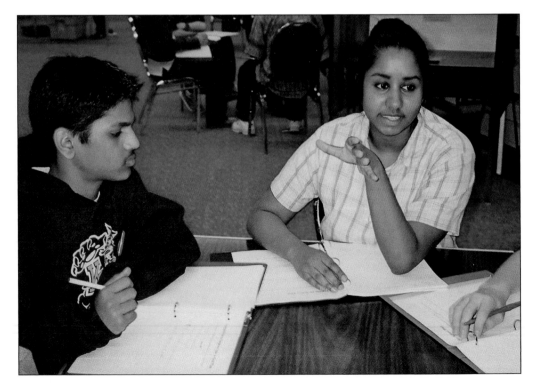

When you are working as part of a team it is important to treat each person with respect, no matter how rushed you might be.

teammates, or we might try to be fair to everyone in a group, but end up not meeting anyone's needs. In situations that pit your values against each other, it's easy to get confused and not know what to do.

Remember, character is putting your values into action as best as you can. All that can be asked is that you do your best. If you still find yourself totally stumped by an ethical dilemma, try one (or more) of the following four Take Action Ethics Tests. They can help clarify a situation and lead you toward an answer that leaves your conscience clear and strengthens your character.

TAKE ACTION ETHICS TESTS

Golden Rule: Are you treating others as you would want to be treated?

Public Scrutiny: Would you be comfortable if your reasoning and final decision were to be publicized on the front page of your local newspaper?

Kid-on-Your-Shoulder: How would you feel if your younger brother or sister were observing you?

Voice of Reason: Would the most ethical person you know applaud your decision?

Take Action!

Using the CARE Model, the Take Action Ethics Tests, and your own judgment, consider how you would deal with the following scenarios. Share your reasoning and final decision with a partner and discuss them. How did your ethical decision-making processes differ? How did the differences affect the outcome? Now try to develop a compromise approach with your partner, and join with another pair to share and discuss the different processes and outcomes.

1 You are among new friends at a party, and the person you have a crush on asks you if you want to go outside together to smoke a joint. You know that this person has had serious problems with drugs in the past, and has been proudly clean for several months. If you discourage this person from using drugs now, you will lose your chance to be alone with him or her and may possibly cause him or her to lose interest in you. What do you do?

2 You and your friend are both interested in the same internship, and you decide to both apply for it. After seeing your friend's résumé, you realize that your friend has a lot more experience than you, so you make up a few things on your own résumé to ensure that you qualify as well. As a result, you are selected for the internship and your friend is not. Do you admit that you were dishonest, when this means that you will lose the work opportunity and perhaps your friend as well?

3 A close friend of yours confesses to you that he or she is contemplating suicide, and then swears you to secrecy. You agree because you want him or her to know that you are trustworthy. If you tell someone, you may lose his or her trust, and possibly make him or her feel more alone. If you keep the secret, your friend's life may be in danger. What do you do?

4 At the start of your summer holidays, you are attending a protest at a factory that supplies the army with weapons that are believed to have horrific, long-term effects on large numbers of innocent people. The police have warned that anyone who trespasses on factory property will receive an automatic, two-month jail sentence. Several people, including one of your friends, begin to climb the gate, but the others say they do not want to jeopardize their summer break, or to have criminal records that may prevent them from getting a job in the future. Do you climb or stay?

5 You are responsible for an anti-terrorism task force that will protect the civilians of your country from harm. You have apprehended a known terrorist and have knowledge that he or she has been involved in planning an attack that is set to occur within days. The terrorist refuses to reveal the plans to you. Someone on the force suggests that torture will force the terrorist to speak. Do you agree and violate the prisoner's human rights because this may save the lives of other people?

> *"That's what I consider true generosity. You give your all and yet you always feel as if it costs you nothing."*
>
> — Simone de Beauvoir (1908–1986)
> Author, philosopher

The Level 3 Leader

Among the young people who work with Free the Children and Leaders Today, there is a concept called "Level 3." It means seeing every choice and every action as a chance to change the world, and realizing that change has to begin with each one of us. Level 3, we believe, is not merely something we do; it is a way of life. Level 3 is the courage to dream, the passion to believe, and the intensity to act. It is the energy that allows us to make the ordinary extraordinary, to change our lives, the lives of others, and the world around us. It means striving to *live our values* every single day as socially conscious and responsible global citizens.

Sound intimidating? Sure it is, and that is why there are also Levels 1 and 2. Level 1 is first becoming socially involved in little ways. This can mean smiling at a student whom others exclude or reject, recycling your plastic water bottle, or refraining from telling and laughing at racist jokes. Level 2 is taking your commitment to a higher level in your thoughts, actions, and words. It may include speaking to a student whom others exclude or reject, refilling your plastic bottle with drinking water for a month, or objecting when you hear a racist joke.

When you are ready and committed and psyched — we mean really ready, really committed, and really psyched — you can "punch it up a click" to Level 3. Level 3 means doing things that most people would never dream of doing, and that some people would even make fun of you for — but remembering that everything you do is part of something bigger, and that there is no time off from your values or how you live your life. Level 3 may include inviting that student whom others exclude on a social outing with you and your friends, organizing a drive in the cafeteria for reusable bottles, or setting up a team to organize a multicultural event in your school.

No matter what level you are operating on (and it will change from day to day, moment to moment, depending on how much sleep you've had or if you have a test next period), you are changing the world. Our challenge to you, though, is to be more at Level 3 more of the time, as much as you can!

PROFILE Joe Opatowski: A Leader

Growing up, Joe Opatowski was a class clown who scored high marks and was involved in volunteer work, but his heart was not always in it. The fighting in his family seemed to drown out everything else in his life. On the outside, Joe pretended that things were fine, but deep down he was beginning to crumble. Desperate for a way out, he began using and dealing marijuana.

When Joe was 15, he made contact with Free the Children, and was given the opportunity to volunteer in Riverton, Jamaica, a town built inside a garbage dump. There, he met children who suffered from malnutrition but who wanted to grow up to do incredible things. Joe knew that he had nothing to offer them but his time and energy, but he gave it purely, and from the heart. Giving them piggyback rides and watching their faces light up, he realized how intimately his own happiness was connected to theirs. He discovered that helping people know that life was worth living was what brought meaning to his own life.

When he returned home, Joe realized that he had some serious things to figure out. He knew that he could not go back to dealing drugs if he wanted to be a mentor and empower young people to change the world. He gave up drugs for good and decided to move out on his own.

Taking care of himself was not always easy. Joe was forced to take on a couple of dismal jobs, working in restaurants and bars and telemarketing at night, while still going to school during the day. It was difficult, but he took solace in the fact that he was finally taking control of his life — despite the sadness that he experienced, he was choosing to shape it himself with as much purpose and joy as he could.

Today, as the Leadership Coordinator for Leaders Today, Joe inspires young people every day to make a difference in the lives of others. He is a popular facilitator of workshops — in North America, Ecuador, and Thailand — because of his extraordinary intensity and positive outlook, unique ideas, listening skills, and ability to make everyone he meets believe in themselves. Joe has worked hard to bring these same lessons into his home in order to understand his family better, as they continue to rediscover what they mean to one another.

1 What choices — good and bad — did Joe make on his path toward becoming a leader? How do you evaluate Joe's character? How does he display integrity and courage?

2 Describe a time when you acted at Level 3 (it could be in sports or in school or at home or with friends). How did it feel? What were the consequences, both good and bad, of putting yourself on the line? Was it worth it?

3 Whom in your life do you look up to for their courage and integrity? What qualities do they display that make you admire their character?

The Seven Steps to Social Action: Taking It to the Next Level

CONTENTS

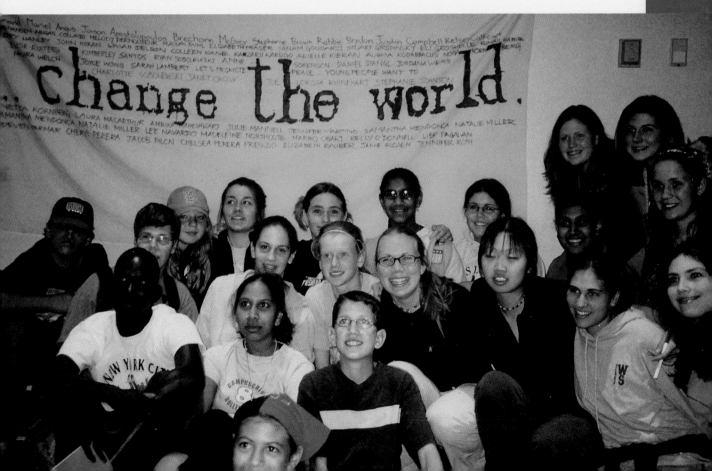

Turning Passion Into Action

In April 2001, over 35 000 people poured into the streets of Québec City to voice their views at the opening of a new round of global trade negotiations. Among them were students, teachers, clergy, social workers, small business owners, farm workers, feminists, environmentalists, and others from every kind of background. They stood together in solidarity for fair labour standards, environmental protection, and basic human rights.

Young people made up nearly one third of the crowd. The protesters sang, chanted, blew whistles, shook tambourines, and danced to the beat of drums. There were jugglers among them, stilt walkers, mimes, and puppeteers. Their spirit was as strong as their statement, and their commitment to the issue was clear. They were protesting the inequalities of globalization and standing up for human rights everywhere.

Were you among them, on that day? Do you wish you had been? Are these issues that you care about too? The good news is that you don't have to go to a protest somewhere far away or spend a day on stilts to change the world. As a global citizen, you can start taking action in your classroom, your community, and even right in your home. It all begins with a dream and a daily effort, as Noam Chomsky, a famous activist, writer, and linguist from the Massachusetts Institute of Technology (MIT) wrote:

There are no magic answers, no miraculous methods to overcome the problems we face, just the familiar ones: honest search for understanding, education, organization, action.

The path to change that Chomsky describes is simple and direct. It reveals the steps followed by social activists everywhere who know that a better world will come when we work hard to create it. Global citizens around the world use the steps outlined in this section to break down complex, overwhelming issues into small, manageable actions that turn their *passion* into *concrete social change*. If you want to make a difference, these steps will show you how.

THE SEVEN STEPS TO SOCIAL ACTION

1 Find your passion

2 Research the reality

3 Build your dream team

4 Meet around the round table

5 Set a mission

6 Take action!

7 Bring in the fun!

Whether you are experienced as an active global citizen, or just beginning, you can use the Seven Steps to help you

Young people at the Québec City protest stand with their mouths taped shut, in solidarity with those who are forced to suffer in silence from the negative effects of globalization.

focus your efforts, overcome obstacles, and put creative solutions into action. No matter what your issue or level of commitment, from getting healthier options at your cafeteria to fighting AIDS in Africa, you can follow these Seven Steps to reach your goals!

Step 1: Find Your Passion

A great fire begins with a small spark. Every social movement begins the same way, when one person's passion lights up a crowd.

Passion is about finding your purpose, what inspires and awakens something inside you. Every person has an issue that is close to the heart — something that makes him or her angry, frustrated, or sad; a pet peeve or a news story that hurts to watch. Sometimes we discover it suddenly, like one of the authors, Craig Kielburger, did when he was flipping through the newspaper looking for the comics one morning and instead saw a headline that changed his life: "Battled Child Labour, Boy 12, Murdered!" Being 12 years old himself at the time, Craig felt an instant connection to the story of the boy in Pakistan. He had never heard about the issue of child labour before that day, but he knew he had to do something to help.

What is it that moves you? Think about your own life and the problems that you see. Have you ever:

- Experienced or witnessed racism or discrimination because of gender, age, height, weight, clothes, appearance, or any other reason?

- Noticed garbage littering the parks that you spend time in?

- Felt unsafe walking home alone at night?

- Lost a nearby wooded area because of a new building development or housing project?

- Read an article or seen a television program that made you say, "That's not right!" or "Why do people let that happen?"

Many people around the world face the same struggles. Social issues, such as racism, poverty, pollution, and conflict, are global, even though they may vary in severity in different regions. It is important to understand the *global* reach of these problems, but our actions can target their *local* occurrences. When you *think globally and act locally*, you work at the level of real solutions, where you can see an immediate and definite impact.

Think globally and act locally

- If you want to end world poverty, you might start by gathering a group of friends to distribute food and health items to the homeless in your city, *or* order some extra food when dining out and take it "to go" to give to someone who asks you for change on the street, *or* organize a clothing drive for people in need in your community.

- If you want to promote fair labour standards, you can become involved in the No Sweat Campaign. This campaign ensures that clothes that bear your school's logo are not made through exploitative practices. You can cut out the labels from the clothes that you buy and include them in letters to the companies that

> "The greatest thing you can do for another is not just share your riches, but reveal to them their own."
>
> — Benjamin Disraeli (1804–1881) English Statesman, former Prime Minister of Great Britain

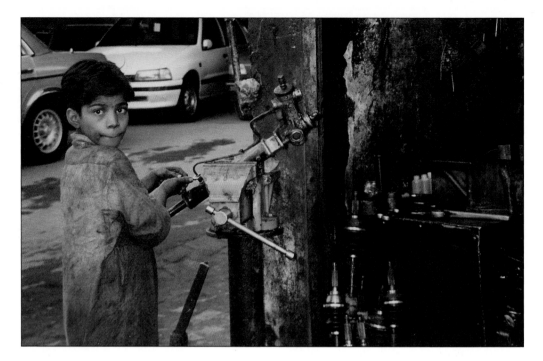

A young boy works to repair a vehicle in a mechanics shop in India. Children involved in this type of work are often exposed to dangerous and exploitative conditions.

make them. You can inform the companies that you will not buy any more clothing from them until you see a copy of their codes of conduct and are satisfied that their labour standards are acceptable.

- If you are concerned about the issues of war and intolerance, you can organize a workshop on the human realities of a recent war and present it to your school, or you can make friends with a student of a different culture from yours.

- If you are concerned about global warming, you can start a bike co-op in your community; you and your friends can fix up old bikes and sell them cheaply to promote sustainable transportation. Or, write a letter to encourage your local authorities to establish or improve bike lanes or the public transit system.

It doesn't matter how you start making a difference; just as these issues are global, they are all interconnected. For example, the poverty of many communities around the world is a result of unfair global trade policies or consumer demand for cheap food and products. And the inequalities and injustices produced by these factors are often at the root of violence and war.

It is important to understand that social problems are interconnected and inseparable. But working for change does not require tackling all of these problems at once. It means, rather, that by working on one problem, you are really working on all of them! At the core, what counts is that you are involved and that you care. Choose an issue that is meaningful to you. This is the key to unlocking your passion and to starting a project that you are committed to seeing through.

Global Issues at a Glance

Unsure of what issue to choose? This section will give you a glimpse of some of the most challenging problems our world faces today. What you discover here may inspire you to expand your knowledge by doing your own research into one of these social problems, or finding another issue that really moves you. Check out the Sources and Resources in Part 5 for organizations that are working on these issues. You can contact them for more information and for ideas on how to get involved.

Demonstrators in Québec City, 2001 come up with creative ways to voice their views about globalization. This papier maché puppet shows the world in the control of those with political and economic power.

GLOBALIZATION/POVERTY

Globalization refers to the process by which the world is becoming more interconnected in areas such as trade, labour, and technology. This phenomenon has its advantages. We are becoming more aware of other cultures and problems around the world, and we are able to share ideas and resources toward reaching a higher standard of living. However, the benefits of globalization are not equally distributed, and evidence suggests that the gap between rich and poor countries is widening. The 2002 World Summit on Sustainable Development reported that 15% of the world's population living in high-income countries consumes 56% of Earth's resources, while the poorest 40%, in low-income countries, consumes only 11% of its resources.

In today's globalized economy, many of the products we buy are produced by multinational corporations (MNCs). In order to keep costs down and remain competitive, many MNCs have moved factories out of developed nations and into developing nations, where wages are often exploitatively low, worker safety regulations are few, and environmental laws are frequently neglected. Increased production and consumption have serious environmental consequences, which include deforestation, increased levels of carbon dioxide emissions, and contamination of water sources and other natural resources.

SUBSTANCE ABUSE

Youth are exposed to a variety of mixed messages about drugs, alcohol, and tobacco. The media often portrays these substances as attractive, and some of your peers may dismiss them as harmless, and even positive for your status or image. In Canada, more than 60% of university students and 25% of high school students binge drink on a routine basis (5 or more drinks per occasion). This trend comes with a consequence. MADD (Mothers Against Drunk Driving) estimates that 1690 Canadians die and 74 000 are injured each year in alcohol-related crashes, and roughly 50% of all violent crimes in Canada involve either an offender or a victim who has been drinking. Smoking is another popular but fatal habit. According to Health Canada, tobacco smoke kills over 45 000 people in Canada each year. That's roughly one death every 12 minutes — more than the total of all murders, alcohol-related deaths, car accidents, and suicides.

The use of alcohol, tobacco, and illegal drugs among youth is often linked to depression and trouble in school. **Substance abuse** has also been linked to teenage pregnancies, unwanted or unsafe sex, and the contraction of sexually transmitted diseases such as HIV/AIDS. Users of alcohol and drugs hurt not only themselves, but also those who care about them, and those who share their communities. Substance abuse burdens the economy and the health care system, causes family problems, and leads to crime and violence associated with drug trafficking. It affects the safety and well-being of the entire population of countries throughout the world.

PEACE AND DEMOCRACY

Many people argue that war is inevitable, despite the fact that it is the result of a conscious human choice to kill. According to the Stockholm International Peace Research Institute, in 2002, global military spending reached nearly $800 billion for the first time in history. Less than 1% of this money could give every child in the world a primary school education. Worse yet, at the turn of the twentieth century, 10% of war deaths and injuries were suffered by non-military personnel, and in the new, brutal warfare that marked the turn of the twenty-first century, 90% of casualties are innocent women and children.

True sustainable peace cannot be achieved merely by suppressing conflict. It can be realized only through the active presence of justice. In many countries today, war is connected to the absence of equality and democracy. Many wars are long-standing conflicts relating to ethnic, religious, or national hatreds, but, more than ever, money (the extreme lack of it or the quest for more power and profit) and resources (such as diamonds and oil) command armies. It is clear that democratic societies are more likely to be peaceful, because people are secure and free to contribute to their society. When people are not allowed to participate, they feel disempowered, and this can become the foundation for conflict and civil war. Democracy means challenging ourselves to accommodate differences, through negotiation, dialogue, and the pursuit of equality. We must strive for sustainable peace not only among nations, but also within them, among groups and individuals.

CHILD POVERTY IN CANADA

Children living in prosperous countries are not necessarily free from poverty. In 1989, the Canadian House of Commons made a unanimous resolution to eliminate child poverty by the year 2000. However, according to *Campaign 2000 Report Card*, the number of poor children has actually increased by 21% since then, with 1 in 6 children in Canada living below the poverty line. That is over 1.1 million children, or 16.5% of the population under 18. Over 50% of these children are Aboriginal or from other visible minority groups.

Statistics Canada reports that while children make up 26% of Canada's

"Pacifism simply is not a matter of calm looking on; it is work, hard work."

— Käthe Kollwitz
(1867–1945)
Sculptor, graphic artist

population, they account for 40% of food bank users. Canadian children forced to live in poverty experience more physical and mental health problems than is the norm, often go hungry, and are more likely to live in dangerous neighbourhoods.

The 2000 *UNICEF Report: Child Poverty in Rich Nations* found that wealthy European countries, such as Sweden and Norway, have economies that resemble Canada's, yet have much lower rates of child poverty. These countries put more money toward helping families with children, by investing in income security and unemployment benefits, affordable housing, and accessible child care.

YOUTH VIOLENCE AND CRIME

An alarming number of young people are exposed to or are resorting to violence, in the form of assaults, fights, threats, bullying, gang violence, destruction of property, or date violence. According to Statistics Canada, young people accounted for 21% of those charged with Criminal Code offences in 1999, while representing only 8% of the Canadian population. In Canada, 40% of youth were victims of at least one crime in 1998. Youth 15 to 19 years of age had higher rates of both violent crime and personal theft than did older Canadians.

Young offenders often have other issues that have put them at risk. Some turn to crime as a survival or escape tactic from problems such as poverty, homelessness, or domestic violence. Many of the inequalities that contribute to crime in the first place also carry over into the justice system. Overall, youth of racial or ethnic minorities in Canada are more likely than white youth to be sent to detention and corrections facilities and to be transferred to adult court — often for the same offences. Sometimes, teens feel they are automatically viewed as criminals. Much of public perception is shaped by the media, which often focuses more on youth offences than on youth achievements. Teens who lose respect for a society that ignores them or labels them as trouble may disconnect themselves even further from this society by turning to delinquent behaviour.

SUSTAINABLE CONSUMPTION AND THE ENVIRONMENT

Our planet Earth is an amazing place. Its ecosystems possess a natural balance in which the elements of air, water, land, and plant and animal habitats co-exist and support one another. However, these systems are not invincible. As humans overload Earth with toxins and chemicals, the stability of the planet as a whole is being disrupted. Because the elements of our environment are so interconnected, the damage has a ripple effect, spreading among the atmosphere, soil, waters, and living species.

The over-consumption by industrialized nations is depleting Earth's resources. Many of the world's forests have been destroyed, and what remains of the rainforests is quickly being cleared for agriculture, livestock grazing, and logging to produce the products that we use every day, such as timber, paper, and oil. This deforestation reduces the absorption of greenhouse gases, and can lead to flooding, soil erosion, and changing rainfall and temperature. If the destruction

> "We must talk about poverty, because people insulated by their own comfort lose sight of it."
>
> — Dorothy Day (1897–1980) Journalist, reformer

Remaining elephant habitat is increasingly encroached upon by human settlement and agriculture, leaving many elephant populations restricted to isolated protected areas.

continues at this pace, nearly all tropical rainforests could be lost to us by the year 2030, and half of the world's plant and animal species could be extinct within a century.

RACISM

Racism is a set of unjustified or oversimplified beliefs about a group of people based on their racial or ethnic origin, often as perceived through physical attributes (such as skin colour). Attitudes of fear, hate, or resentment toward the group in question are frequently part of a racist ideology. Along with the differentiation comes the assumption that one group is superior to, or should hold power over, another. When racist attitudes are expressed through actions, this is called "discrimination."

Throughout history, racism has resulted in slavery, anti-immigration legislation, civil rights violations (i.e., denial of access to voting, education, or employment), apartheid, and genocide. According to Human Rights Watch, more than 250 million people in the world today suffer under a form of apartheid, modern-day slavery, or other extreme forms of discrimination because they were born into a marginalized class. Around the globe, refugees, migrants, and internally displaced persons are the victims of racial discrimination and violence — with racism as both the cause and the result of forced displacement. Over the past decade, many industrialized nations have introduced a series of restrictive policies targeting asylum seekers, refugees, and migrants. Members of minority groups in these countries often face harassment, arbitrary detention, and abusive treatment by the justice system.

EXPLOITATION OF CHILDREN

Millions of children around the world are forced into exploitative activities, and are robbed of their health, their innocence, their dignity, and their right to simply enjoy being a child. The International Labour Organization estimates that there are nearly 250 million children working worldwide, half of them full time, labouring on farms or plantations, selling items on the streets, or performing domestic chores in other people's homes. The commercial sexual exploitation of children (including child prostitution and pornography) is estimated to be a multi-billion dollar industry, drawing in over one million children a year worldwide. And over 300 000 children under 18 are currently serving as soldiers in government or armed rebel groups, forced to commit horrific acts of violence against their own communities.

The United Nations Convention on the Rights of the Child, ratified by 192 UN member countries, including Canada, declares that children have the right to be kept safe from neglect, cruelty, and exploitation. Yet children are being exploited in every country in the world. The situation is most critical in developing regions, where poor and marginalized children (especially girls and ethnic minorities) are among the most vulnerable.

ABORIGINAL RIGHTS

While Canada has long been rated one of the best countries in the world in which to live, there is a great discrepancy in living standards between its Aboriginal and non-Aboriginal populations. Most Aboriginal people live at or below the poverty line, and have unemployment rates that are two to three times the Canadian rate. They have a life expectancy that is six years shorter than the Canadian average, and an infant mortality rate that is double the national average. Housing on Aboriginal reserves is frequently inadequate and in short supply, with substandard water and sewage systems. Indian and Northern Affairs Canada reports that Aboriginal Canadians experience poorer

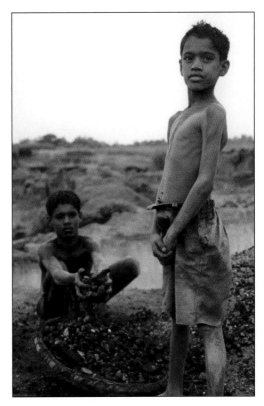

Labouring in a quarry, children such as these are often underpaid and mistreated by their overseers. They are also likely to suffer long-term health problems such as stunted growth and respiratory disorders due to exposure to heavy loads and toxic fumes.

health, and higher incidences of HIV/ AIDS, diabetes, substance abuse, and family violence. Aboriginal youth in Canada are also less likely to graduate from high school and go on to post-secondary education, more likely to spend time in jail, and at least twice as likely to commit suicide as other Canadian youth.

Many of these disintegrating social conditions can be attributed to the discrimination and human rights violations that Aboriginal populations have suffered, not only in Canada, but also in many other regions of the world. Historically, they have had their ancestral lands seized by settlers and colonizers, and degraded by industrialization. Their identities have been similarly attacked, as governments have failed to respect the distinct economic and social organizations, laws, and worldviews of Aboriginal populations.

This has threatened their survival and the preservation of their language, customs, and spirituality.

HIV/AIDS

HIV (human immunodeficiency virus) is a contagious virus that gradually breaks down the immune system, weakening the body's ability to fight infection and disease. The final stage of HIV is called AIDS (acquired immune deficiency syndrome). Many people with AIDS will die from various illnesses that their immune system is unable to combat. AIDS is a pandemic, a disease causing great concern in every country of the world. Almost 22 million people around the globe have died from the virus, with 90% of AIDS cases occurring in developing countries, and 75% concentrated in sub-Saharan Africa. According to the 2002 AIDS Epidemic Update, there were 42 million people living with HIV/AIDS during that year. The pandemic is deepening the poverty of entire communities, with children often being the first to feel the consequences.

HIV/AIDS cannot be spread through casual contact. It may be transmitted through the exchange of bodily fluids in sexual contact, or by sharing infected needles and syringes. A mother can also pass the virus on to her child during pregnancy, childbirth, or breastfeeding. Of the cases in 2002, 3.2 million were in children under 15; and over 90% of them were babies born to HIV-positive women. UNAIDS (the Joint United Nations Programme on HIV/AIDS) reports that over 14 million children have been orphaned as a result of the disease. Because AIDS is closely related to aspects of sexuality that are considered taboo in many cultures and religions, people continue to react to it with fear, resentment, or denial, which presents a challenge to awareness and prevention initiatives.

TAKING ON THE CHALLENGE

Did any of these issues leap out at you and move you to take action? If not, keep searching to find a need or an injustice that stirs something inside you. The problems described here are not small, but they can be overcome. Throughout this book, you will meet several young people, just like you, who are using their talents, vision, and determination to create effective solutions to such problems. As you read their stories, you'll see that change can begin and grow from a single person, a single idea, a single hope for a better future.

There exist limitless possibilities for change that have not even been explored yet. Every young person has the potential to come up with a unique solution — a new way to make a difference. What will yours be?

CHOOSE YOUR ISSUE!

Choose one issue from those on pages 37–42 or come up with one of your own — the one about which you are *most passionate*. We will refer to your chosen issue throughout the rest of the book, so make sure it's one that you really care about. Write it down and remember it. From here on, we will equip you with the tools and skills to make a difference, before you get to the end of the book, and beyond.

PROFILE Alex Apostol: Youth Activist

When he was 14, Alex Apostol became involved with Free the Children and joined its members in handing out food and basic living kits to homeless people in downtown Toronto. He noticed that many of those sitting on the sidewalks with their sleeping bags were his own age. Struck by how their realities contrasted with his own, Alex began talking with the street youth he encountered, wanting to know more about their lives. What he learned was that many were not sleeping on the streets because they were delinquent, but because they simply had no other choice. Some had run away from abuse at home or struggled with psychological problems, and had nowhere to turn for support. Their situations often trapped them in cycles of poverty and depression, which sometimes led to involvement with drugs or prostitution. Many street youth felt that no one understood what they were going through. People walked past them on the street without making eye contact, refusing to acknowledge their presence.

As he learned more about the situation of street youth in Toronto, Alex knew he had to take concerted action to urge others in his city to tackle the issue at its root. Now 19 years old, he is working to encourage the youth of his generation not only to recognize the inequalities and the suffering in their communities, but also to take ownership of these problems. Through his participation in a Leaders Today program called Volunteer Now, Alex facilitates leadership workshops for students throughout Toronto, motivating them not only to achieve their 40-hour community service requirement, but to also push beyond it — by making the experience personal.

Alex has noticed an increased popularity in campaigns to distribute supplies to the homeless, like the ones in which he had been so involved. Empowered by leadership workshops, students are taking on increasingly visible and far-reaching initiatives, such as lobbying and advocacy for affordable housing for the homeless. Alex feels that the solution to poverty lies not only in donating money, but also in changing the structures and conditions at the root of the problem. Beginning in their own neighbourhoods in ways that tap into their own interests, youth like Alex are the foundation of what it will take to address inequalities, both around the world and down the street.

1 Alex began to take a real interest in the issue of homelessness in his city when he discovered that many of the homeless were youth his own age. Do you think it is important to identify with an issue in order to want to help? Explain.

2 Try to imagine yourself in the position of a street youth. Write a paragraph describing how you would feel if someone walked past you and refused to look at you. Write another paragraph describing how you would want and deserve to be treated.

3 Which problems do you feel are more important to address: those in countries overseas, or those in your own community? Explain your answer.

STAYING PSYCHED: PASSION BOOSTERS

To stay dedicated to your issue every single day, remember why you got involved. This is the fuel that gets you psyched up to push toward your goal with true passion. But it may be hard to remember your mission as you wake up in the morning or after a long day at school. Give yourself visible, tangible reminders of your mission that stir your memory and rekindle your passion to work harder. Your **passion booster** can be a sad picture of a child soldier or a polluted river, or a beautiful picture of the world that you dream of. It can be a ring or necklace you were given by someone special who shares your cause, or a quotation or poem you stick on your bathroom mirror or locker. Your passion boosters can give you an instant rush of adrenalin to do whatever it takes to accomplish your goals.

Choose a passion booster that inspires you. It could be a beautiful image, such as this rainbow.

Take Action!

1 List some of the issues that you see around your school and community. Choose three, and brainstorm four actions you can take to make a difference: two small, one medium, and one hard.

2 Ask two friends what issues they are passionate about. Are they different from or the same as yours? Brainstorm simple ways you can all make a difference.

Step 2: Research the Reality

You may have heard this expression before, but pay special attention this time, because without it, your quest for a better world ends right here: *Knowledge is power.* If you want to make a difference, you have to educate yourself. You have to know what you are striving for.

Research plays a key role in any movement for social justice. It lays the groundwork for your actions in three main ways. First, it reveals the facts about an issue. You have to know what the problem is, where and why it is happening, who is involved, and what impact it has, on whom. Secondly, it allows you to communicate this information to others and to rally a team to the cause. And thirdly, it enables you to find appropriate solutions and devise effective strategies to put them in place.

Finding solutions to social issues is far more difficult than it seems. You have to learn about not only the current state of the problem, but its root causes as well — the historical, political, economic, and social factors that gave rise to and perpetuated it. Because many of the world's problems are the result of years of discrimination and injustice, becoming familiar with the background

is a crucial step to developing lasting solutions. As you learn more about the kinds of solutions that have been attempted in the past, you can evaluate their successes and failures to find an improved and effective plan of action.

Research also motivates you to strive harder to succeed and inspire others to become involved; the more you learn about an issue, the stronger your emotional reaction and passion to make a difference. Knowing the complete reality of an issue is even more important when you are speaking out and taking action as a young person. Because of your age, people may be tempted to dismiss you as naïve, idealistic, or uneducated. In fact, it is often ten times harder to earn credibility as a young person. Your opponents may want to tell you that you do not know what you are talking about. Prove them wrong! Show them that young people have the power to make a difference and that your passion and belief in a better world is rooted in a solid and realistic understanding of the issues and how they can be solved. The chart on page 46 will help you determine how to conduct your research.

Once you have the information you want, you have to know how to document it. The process is called "citation," which is, basically, the act of writing down the source of the information. A

Tip

Beware when researching and citing statistics. The wording is just as important as the numbers, so understand *exactly* what the numbers represent. You also need to make sure that your source is reliable.

Tip

Be very cautious when interviewing individuals you do not know. Avoid being alone with someone by bringing along at least two friends, or by carrying out surveys or interviews in public places in daylight.

What Are You Looking For?

Type of Information	How You Can Use It	Where to Find It
Facts	*What* is the problem, *where* is it happening, *when* does/did it happen, *why* is it a problem and *why* does it happen, *who* is involved and *whom* does it affect, and *how* does it affect you, your community, and the world?	• Daily newspapers • Brochures or Web sites of organizations involved in the issue • The people who are involved and directly affected • Backgrounder sections of network and television news station Web sites
Statistics	"Stats" can give you an idea of the *scope* (size and trends) of the issue. Try to put them into a context that you and others can relate to. For example: • 130 million children around the world are denied the chance to go to school. That is equivalent to every child in North America and Europe being denied any schooling. • Every year, 25 million people die of hunger. That's almost 70 000 a day.	• UN organizations' yearly reports • Brochures or Web sites of organizations involved in the issue • Statistics Canada • Special issues of magazines on the subject • Your own surveys
Stories	Facts and statistics are powerful in convincing people that there is a problem, but numbers can be overwhelming and do not often inspire an emotional reaction. What really convinces people to take action on an issue is a captivating story. True accounts of people affected by an issue reveal the human face of a problem, ensuring an emotional connection, both for the people you are trying to convince, and for you.	• Interviews with people affected by the issue or others who know them • Video documentaries (they have their own section in video stores, and are often on CBC, PBS, provincial public television, or the Documentary Channel)

citation looks like a bibliography reference. Make sure you record the name of the writer; the title and type (book, film, newspaper) of the source; the year the information was published or the date of the airing (if television or radio), interview, survey, or letter; and the page number or exact address of the Web site. When you are thinking of publishing your research, libraries usually offer many different style guides for writing citations. In the meantime, just make sure you have all your citations written down and safely kept with all of your research. It is often easiest to have the citation on the same page as the research to avoid looking all over for it.

Any one source will not provide you with all the information you require, because you need to consider various perspectives. Even if the first one seems totally reliable it is important to consult a number of different sources and cross-check the information to determine where it agrees and where it conflicts. Considering the issue from different points of view will help you to cultivate a broad perspective, and learn to distinguish fact, opinion, and propaganda in what you read and hear. This advice may seem like common sense, but many social action groups have been destroyed by their critics because they have not considered the other side of the issue, or have acquired false or unverified information. It's a lot of work, but it's worth the effort to be thorough in your research. You will be far more effective at finding the *real* solutions if you understand the realities inside and out.

PROFILE Cheryl Perera: Child Rights Activist

Cheryl Perera had always known that she wanted to help people, but was not sure how. She had never felt a real connection to any specific cause until, through her research for a high school project, she came across the issue of child exploitation. Her reading soon revealed that Sri Lanka, her family's home country, was a region in which child labour had become rampant. The discovery left Cheryl feeling very disturbed. She decided that she wanted to work to expose this reality by gathering research and documentation.

When she began to talk about her plans to go to Sri Lanka, people around her found plenty of reasons why it was a bad idea: she had never been there before; it was too controversial; it was too risky. But Cheryl persisted, and finally convinced her parents to let her go — she would travel with an aunt and stay with relatives. A few days after arriving in Sri Lanka, Cheryl and a family member visited a number of quarries that used dynamite. Her reading had not prepared her for the sight of children perched on high ladders, chipping limestone with hammers, and rolling heavy stones into carts. Children as young as five were working dangerously close to the blasts, covered in white dust. Cheryl captured these scenes with her video camera, and became more determined than ever to do something about what she saw.

In the following weeks, Cheryl worked with local human rights organizations to compile a list of recommended actions to address issues such as child labour, prostitution, and domestic servitude, which they presented to the President's advisor. Their suggestions included allocating more of the national budget to child protection, appointing labour inspectors, and considering the input of child victims themselves when developing programs that affect them. Because of her first-hand knowledge, Cheryl was able to understand and communicate the hardships faced by these children. She plans to return to Sri Lanka in the near future to help form a Children's Parliament that would promote children's rights.

Cheryl's experiences in Sri Lanka gave her a close understanding of how exploited children are forced to compromise their identities and values. Since her return to Canada, she has given many presentations to youth groups about the problem of child exploitation. The images and stories she carried home have made her a very passionate speaker and continue to move her and her audiences to action.

1 Why was research crucial in inspiring Cheryl to take action on the issue of the exploitation of children? In your opinion, why is sharing the story of what she witnessed in Sri Lanka effective in motivating others to act?

2 What are the obstacles and risks that one might encounter in trying to visit sites such as factories to document an exploitative practice such as child labour?

3 Make a list of precautions to take when attempting to gather research in this manner. What other ways are there to obtain this type of first-hand testimony?

FINDING THE ROOT CAUSES OF YOUR ISSUE

In order to find a solution to any social issue, you need to evaluate its root causes. It is important to dig deep and find out why the problem exists and why it has yet to be solved. Unfortunately, people often react to social issues by focussing on solutions before exploring the causes of the problem. This approach only covers up the problem and often makes it far worse. For example, the typical approach to overfilling garbage dumps is often to ship the garbage to another city (or even another country!), to dump it into an abandoned mineshaft, or to burn it in large, polluting incinerators. These methods do not consider how we could reduce the amount of garbage we produce or how to convince people to reuse and recycle.

Let's take the issue of child labour as another example. Many young people ask us at Free the Children which companies to boycott to put an end to child labour. They do not realize, however, that only 5% of child labour is in the export industry (in which children manufacture goods to be sold in other countries). Boycotts thus only touch the surface of the problem and are not always the best solution. There are many other root causes of exploitative child labour that must be addressed. Some of these are shown in the chart below.

An effective solution to child labour is one that addresses each of the root causes and considers the perspectives of all stakeholders (individuals who are involved directly and indirectly in the issue). Only solutions that address all perspectives and stakeholders can result in positive change that is meaningful and lasting.

Child Labour: Stakeholders

- National governments can ratify and enforce the International Labour Organization's Convention 182 on the worst forms of child labour. They can pass and enforce legislation that guarantees all workers a livable wage and invest more money in education programs.

- International governments can increase aid to developing countries, especially for education programs, and eliminate unfair trade policies and high interest rates on debts.

- Corporations can pay taxes and give back to countries where they are getting cheap labour, in the form of programs for children. If all companies paid their adult workers a livable wage and provided good

> "Once social change begins, it cannot be reversed. You cannot uneducate the person who has learned to read. You cannot humiliate the person who feels pride. You cannot oppress the people who are not afraid anymore."
>
> — César Chávez (1927–1993) Labour leader

Root Causes of Child Labour

Poverty	→ exploitation of children and poor people; homelessness; migration from rural areas; high interest rate on loans
Education	→ illiteracy; lack of schools, qualified teachers, and supplies; poor school programs
Discrimination	→ based on sex, religion, ethnic background, traditions
Economic and political realities	→ national budgets with few social programs; unfair trade policies; high interest rates on debts; conflicts and war
Globalization	→ free-flowing capital; jobs moving to cheapest markets; exploitation of workers in poor countries; corporations escaping taxes, with loss of revenue for social programs
Sweatshop labour	→ adults who are not paid a living wage for their work must force their children to work in the informal sector (on the streets, as domestic servants, in agriculture) to help the family survive

When researching a complex issue, it's a good idea to work as a team. Divide up different aspects of the issue, and then share what you have learned with one another.

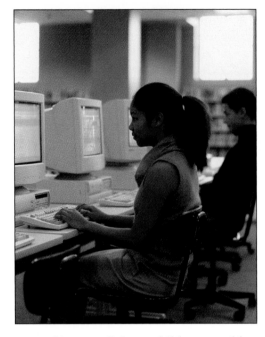

their children, including informal education centres for children who work part-time.

• Child labourers who become literate and aware of their rights when provided with an education can break the cycle of poverty and exploitation. Older child labourers can take a stand against exploitation and organize for fair working conditions, with hours adapted so that they have time for education and leisure.

• Young people around the world can continue to speak out against the exploitation of children and promote the right of all children to go to school and to grow up in a safe and healthy environment.

working conditions, children would not be forced to work.

• Parents earning a livable wage or who are provided with an alternative source of income would be able to send their children to school.

• Non-Governmental Organizations (NGOs) or foreign aid can help families to develop income-generating projects and schools for

When doing your research and seeking out organizations that focus on your issue, you may want to ask them how their proposed solutions address root causes and the perspectives of all stakeholders involved. This will allow you to evaluate the effectiveness of their projects and campaigns, and guide you as you begin to develop your own.

Take Action!

1 Compile one page of facts, several key statistics, and two stories for your issue. Write them down (don't forget citations!). Use this information to try to convince one friend or family member to get involved in your issue.

2 Brainstorm all the root causes of your chosen issue (see page 42). You may need to do some significant research before being able to compile a full list.

3 Research all the potential stakeholders in your chosen issue and evaluate their role in creating the change you wish to see.

Step 3: Build Your Dream Team

As one global citizen, you can certainly make a difference. You can research an issue and make a powerful presentation about it on your own. You can pick up litter in the local park. You can write letter after letter to a public official to pressure for a change in policy. But imagine what can be done if your entire class got involved and devoted all their time and energy to writing letters as well. What if all the students in your school, and every other school in your community, in your province, across Canada, combined their efforts? Imagine the mountain of letters that would make, and how much harder it would be for officials to ignore the message they contained.

That's impossible, you're probably thinking. But it's not. In fact, it's the way Free the Children got started. From a small group of young people in Thornhill, Ontario, the organization has grown into a worldwide network, having involved over one million youth in its projects.

The key to social action is teamwork. It's simple: When you are surrounded by people who are committed to your cause, you can accomplish a lot more. Team members, each with their own gifts, help to make the effort more powerful and meaningful. They encourage and support one another, and remind you of why you first became involved. Many of the great movements for social change were born when individuals discovered a common purpose. In fact, without this shared process, there can be no real *movements*. How effective would the Million Man March on Washington for civil rights in 1995 have been with only one guy walking down the street?

So you have your issue and your research. Can you find a hundred people to join your cause full time, right away? Probably not, but never fear! Most young people try to get dozens of members to all of their meetings, but that is too many to effectively make decisions and move forward. Try the simple strategy that follows to first build a solid Core Group and then find a legion of helpers.

First, we begin with *you*: You are passionate and understand the problem well, and you need help.

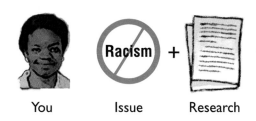

You   Issue   Research

CORE GROUP

Next, we add your **Core Group**: You'll only need three to five people to plan and co-ordinate most of your further research and actions. They must all be very passionate, committed to the cause, and ready to work together on the Dream Team as a high priority in their lives. Look first to your best friends and people involved in your extra-curricular activities — they are likely to share many of your values and thoughts. You could also check out the other social action groups in your school or community such as the student council, leadership council, and other school associations to find people to join your team.

It may remain difficult to get others as involved as you are. So ask yourself:

- Who else is affected by this problem?
- Who is committed to solving it?
- Where can I go to find these people?
- Who is already an activist?
- What specific skills or knowledge am I missing that others can contribute?

You have a whole range of people to consider as potential members of your Core Group. Choose wisely — you will have to trust and depend on these individuals to help you succeed!

Core Group

MINGA TEAM

Finally, we add the *minga*. You will find many people who want to help, but who are too busy with sports, band, drama, or homework to dedicate a lot of time, but they *can* offer an hour a week, or one day every month. These are still very valuable members of your Dream Team. They all have talents, ideas, and energy to share, so sign them up and give them a role to play! Make a list of your Minga Team, with the following info:

- Name
- Contact (phone, e-mail)
- Availability
- Skill, gift, or specific contribution/task such as:

  — Phone calls

  — Donations

  — Posters

  — Event participation

  — Ticket sales

  — Information distribution

  — Running an information booth

  — Petition circulation

  — Letter writing

  — Research

Core Group +

Minga Team

THE MINGA

Many indigenous societies in Central and South America accomplish their biggest projects — like constructing houses or schools, planting large plots of crops, or making clothes and crafts — by holding a *minga*. Everyone leaves his or her own work to come together for one day to work as a whole community. Everyone performs a specific task, and the project is completed in no time! *Mingas* are awesome ways to get big things done quickly, but they are also amazing experiences that promote unity, friendship, and solidarity among community members. These indigenous societies are among the most tightly knit, mutually supportive communities in the world — because of the *minga*!

There you have all the ingredients for your Dream Team — the Core Group meets regularly, plans and co-ordinates actions, and then delegates tasks to the Minga Team for the big actions, whose members carry out the actions all together. Delegating effectively is key to your success, but the secret to organizing your Dream Team is creating a sense of ownership and responsibility for the issue among all members. Your teammates must be as passionate about the issue as you are!

Keep your team inspired

- Always ask for input — appreciate it and implement it.

- Delegate important tasks — not just the easy or unglamorous ones.

- Tap into people's gifts — encourage team members to contribute their special talents and skills.

- Make decisions as a team — try to achieve a consensus (general agreement) whenever possible.

- Make your passion contagious — regularly remind your team of why you are all involved and what the issue is really about. Make your idealism and positive vibes shine!

EMBRACING A DIVERSE COMMUNITY

The key to building a strong group is inclusion. When organizing a group of people who are dedicated to your cause, remember that diversity is an essential and enriching force, not an obstacle. Someone who has had a different experience may see situations in another light and challenge you to broaden your

Troubleshooting

What Happens if No One Wants to Join?

If you are unsure of how to ask people to join your cause, try speaking in front of your class or school. You would be surprised how many people will join just by seeing how passionate you are. Tell your audience exactly what you want: "Join my group," or "Come to our meeting Thursday at 3:15." Do not give up! Some people may need to watch you take action for a while before they come around, but once you have your first few members, the floodgates will open! You can also try speaking to people individually — find out what their skills are and tell them how those skills would be a valuable asset to your team. If you're still having trouble starting a new group, you can always join an existing one and bring your energy and ideas to them. As a new member, you can take initiative and recruit others to the organization, putting your leadership skills to great use.

perspective. When you welcome more diverse voices, their shared purpose will break down traditional boundaries between people, spur new ideas, and build a united effort that promotes peace and solidarity at the same time.

THE FOUR TYPES OF LEADERS

As you build your team, you will have to deal with team dynamics and various people's views on leadership. Your members may fall into different roles that are essential to the workings of a well-oiled team. It is important to understand various leadership styles so that you can fill every role that your team needs to be effective and direct members toward roles that best suit their personal teamwork style.

There are four kinds of leaders: visionaries, doers, reasoners, and bridge-builders. Each leadership type is critical to the success of any team, and can be compared to the parts of a bicycle.

Visionaries are the team's trail guide. They dream and inspire. They develop new ideas and ways of approaching a problem or a task that the team must face. Visionaries are always thinking, brainstorming, suggesting, and painting a picture of where the team should go and what it can accomplish.

Doers are the team's pedals. Their actions set the team in motion. They lead by example, motivating people and maintaining team momentum toward the main goal. Doers are in constant motion, working to push the team's accomplishments forward.

Reasoners are the team's handle-bars. They guide and protect the team from harm. They analyse the team's goals and actions, and decide the best possible way to achieve the goals, given the specific conditions and circumstances. Reasoners do a lot of calculating, analysing, organizing, and budgeting, and they often have to

As you build your group, look for members who vary in cultural background, political orientation, knowledge, experience, skills, age, and ways of life. By comparing perspectives, group members discover the attitudes, values, and concerns that others have about the issue that you all seek to confront.

redirect team members who wander off lost in the woods somewhere. Often, the most quiet and thoughtful people in the group are the most gifted reasoners.

Bridge-builders are the team's gears and chain. They make all of the other parts work together and move in the same direction. They resolve conflicts among the other members of the team to ensure that the team stays focused and on target. Bridge-builders engage in negotiations and problem solving.

Every successful team needs all four kinds of leaders. Ask yourself which role best suits you and makes the most of your gifts and skills.

EXERCISE YOUR LEADERSHIP SKILLS

Working with others is not always easy. Members of even the most solid groups sometimes disagree over strategies, blame one another for mistakes, or clash over different personalities. As a leader, you must do your best to promote the unity of your team by reminding everyone of the purpose that brought all of you together, and ensuring that each individual feels that he or she belongs to the group and has a valuable contribution to make. To avoid conflict and lay the groundwork for an effective team, it is helpful to work together to develop standards of behaviour, or group norms, that you all agree to uphold. Such norms might include not interrupting one another in meetings, taking turns to speak, and respecting the opinions and feelings of every member. Sit down as a group and brainstorm potential norms for everyone to follow, and then vote on each idea. Try to make the decisions as unanimous as possible.

Tip

For more information on developing group norms and resolving conflicts within a group, see the Connecting with People section in the How-To Guide.

Types of Leaders

Type of Leader	A.K.A.	Talents	Tasks
Visionaries	Idea people	• Imagination • Passion • Inventiveness • Courage to dream	• Project proposals and design • Mission statements • Long-term planning • Media relations
Doers	Hands-on people	• Energy • Perseverance • Flexibility • Artistic skills	• Posters and logos • Fundraising • Manual labour • Baking, building, shopping
Reasoners	Detail people	• Organization • Logic • Math and science skills • Street sense	• Budgets • Logistics • Co-ordinating • Reporting to supporters
Bridge-builders	Unifying people	• Compassion • Communication skills • Oratory skills • Listening skills	• Holding team meetings • Giving pep talks • Managing • Mediating

Tip

Seek out adults in your community to join your team as advisors and mentors. They may have valuable knowledge, experience, and skills to contribute to the cause. Try to find individuals who will be supportive of the youth-led nature of your team. These might be parents, teachers, members of other organizations with a similar mandate, or professionals with specific skills who share your passion for the issue.

GREAT WAYS TO BRING OUT THE BEST IN YOUR GROUP

1 Find out which skills each person possesses, and how he or she would be most interested in helping.

2 Find out who has previous leadership experience, who is eager to acquire further leadership skills, and who would prefer to take on a less prominent role.

3 Empower individual members to take the lead in an area in which they feel they can contribute the most.

4 Make sure that all members are enthusiastic about the role that they will play.

5 Ensure that group members treat one another with respect.

6 Share and celebrate small victories.

7 Keep up regular communication.

 ## Troubleshooting

The First Meeting

You will want to start slowly at your first meeting with your Core Group. Do not expect to generate a whole list of actions to do the following week. Allow your team members to get to know one another and exchange knowledge, ideas, and feelings about the issue. Your first meeting is also a great opportunity to get people fired up and committed to the cause.

 ## Take Action!

1 What is your preferred leadership style? Describe a time when you played that role very well.

2 Brainstorm a list of five or six people you could invite to be part of your Core Group for your chosen issue, and a list of places/organizations/people that you could approach to recruit your Minga Team.

3 Now begin to put together your Dream Team! Recruit your Core Group and fill a sign-up sheet with names, contact info, availability, and skills of team members.

Step 4: Meet Around the Round Table

King Arthur and Sir Lancelot had the right idea: Recruit the best knights from across the land (these are your Core Group) and sit them down at a table that has no corners or head — sit down together as equals. The concept of the circular table leads us to the next step — after you define your issue, conduct your research, and build your team, you need to hold a meeting. Your meeting style is crucial to the success of your team for the following reasons:

- It is where team members get to know one another and learn more about the goals and nature of the team.

- It is where research and ideas are shared and developed.

- It is where passion is re-ignited and support is renewed.

- It is where group members get a chance to give direct input.

- It provides a chance for team members to compare experiences, thoughts, and difficulties of their individual tasks and projects.

- It is where team decisions can be made.

- It means a chance to socialize and have fun with your friends afterward.

Of course, you don't actually need a round table to create an environment of equality. As a leader, it is your responsibility to facilitate, or guide, the discussion so that it is focused, productive, and respectful of all participants. It is

Troubleshooting

Showing Your Appreciation

No matter what level of involvement they choose, be sure to show your appreciation for team members, volunteers, and supporters. No effort to make the world a better place can be a true success without the help and support of people who give of themselves and their time. Here are some ways to make your invaluable volunteers feel appreciated:

- Thank them personally and congratulate them on their achievement.
- Hold a volunteer appreciation lunch, dinner, or fun outing.
- Send cards, e-mails, phone calls, pins, or T-shirts that say thank-you!
- Show recognition in project pamphlets, newsletters, banners, or over the morning announcements.

also important to make sure that decisions made during the meeting are understood and supported by the group, that everyone leaves with a task, and that individual commitments are fulfilled, by following up at subsequent meetings. That is the best way to put your ideals into action. A meeting of minds is a catalyst for change. When creative, energetic, and determined people join forces, anything is possible.

You can advertise a larger meeting to gather your Minga Team and other supporters. You could post flyers around your school and community, write an article in the school paper, or include a short message over the morning announcements. If you know students who belong to other organizations, you can ask them to announce your meeting at one of their own. Ensure that you first seek permission to post flyers.

Ask around to find meeting times that avoid scheduling conflicts with other activities. Try early-morning or lunchtime meetings, or get together on the weekend! In your invitation, make sure you tell your recruits about the food and the fun, to make the meeting sound more attractive than doing homework or hanging out at the mall.

BEFORE THE MEETING

Before every meeting make a draft **agenda** — a list of activities you will do and issues you need to discuss during the meeting. You will probably amend it (change the order, or add or subtract items) at the beginning of the meeting based on what participants want to do and discuss. As your team begins to meet regularly, rotate the role of agenda-making among the members of your Core Group. This gives each person the chance to learn how to plan an effective meeting. See below for tips.

MAKING AN AGENDA: THE MENU OF THE MEETING

Agendas are very useful for making sure that your meeting stays on track, accomplishes your goals, and does not go on too long. An agenda is not complicated; it's just an ordered list of activities to do and topics to discuss. Each point on the list is an agenda item. Assign time limits to each item according to how much time you have for the meeting overall. The meeting should range from one to two hours, if you have some fun activities and break-out groups to keep people's interest.

Distribute the draft agenda to people at the beginning of the meeting for their approval. Someone may want to add a topic to discuss, or change a time limit. After the draft agenda has been amended, ask for approval of the agenda by a show of hands. This act means that people accept the agenda and pledge to follow it as the meeting moves along.

The main points on the agenda will be a discussion of your issue and suggested actions. Some other items to include should be the following:

- Amendments to and approval of the agenda

- Icebreakers and introductions

- Questions about the highlights of the last meeting

- Updates from members since the last meeting

- Snack and bathroom breaks (these are *always* longer than you think they will be — overestimate the time limit on this one and you will be just fine!)

- Work time — make posters, share research, practise speeches, plan upcoming events or other activities you can do outside of official meeting space

- Discussion of date, time, place, and roles for the next meeting

- Post-meeting fun

Sample Agenda

AGENDA

Youth Helping Youth Club
Aspiring Heights Secondary School
Meeting Agenda — December 9th, Laiah's house
Facilitator: Kelsey

1. Greetings (by Laiah) (2 min.)
2. Amendments and approval of agenda (3 min.)
3. Icebreaker (by Lauren) (5 min.)
4. Minutes from last meeting (2 min.)
5. Updates from members on their tasks (5 min.)
6. Discussion about kids in poverty in Canada (33 min.)
   Research (from Nisha and Tim)
   Brainstorm solutions
   Action ideas
7. Break! (Smoothies made by Mike!) (10 min.)
8. Break-Out Groups (30 min.)
   Logo drawing
   Poster making for car wash next Saturday
   Research crew (magazines brought by Elizabeth and Mohammed)
   Banner for car wash
9. Reminder of tasks for car wash next Saturday (by Kelly) (5 min.)
10. Next meeting — Date, Time, Place, Roles (5 min.)
11. Meeting adjourns (ends)
12. Pizza!

Post-Meeting Fun! Hike Mount Miguel and Swim (by Ari and Amanda)

> "Ask not what your teammates can do for you. Ask what you can do for your teammates."
>
> — Magic Johnson (b. 1959)
> Professional basketball player

Choose a **facilitator** from your Core Group for the meeting (sometimes known as "moderator" or "chairperson," but the word "facilitator" implies more equality and less control by one person). This person will be responsible for ensuring that group members participate, treat one another respectfully, and follow the agenda. In the event of a conflict, facilitators cannot take sides, but must instead attempt to bring the group to a consensus, in which everyone's opinions and needs are considered. This can be a challenging role, as facilitators sometimes have to remain silent about their own views for the sake of reaching an agreement.

Rotate the responsibility of facilitating among the members of your Core Group for each meeting. This gives everyone a leadership experience.

MAKING MEETINGS FUN

Put the fun back into meetings! Ask someone to prepare an icebreaker (a get-to-know-you game or energizer) to establish a fun, relaxed tone. One icebreaker is the Human Knot. The group forms a circle. Then all members reach into the circle with their right hand and grab someone else's right hand. Then they reach in with their left hand to grab someone else's left hand. The goal is to untangle the group without letting go of hands until the circle is formed again. Because it is a little messy and a lot of fun, the Human Knot quickly puts people at ease.

Make sure you have planned a fun activity for after the meeting, too. A bike ride, pizza and a movie, mini-putt, or bowling are all fantastic ideas to maintain group unity, and to give you something to look forward to after your hard, world-changing work is done!

Ask someone to assume responsibility for recording the minutes of the meeting. The minutes serve as a record of what was discussed at the meeting. They help to clarify the reasons for which decisions were made, inform absent members about what went on, and remind all participants of their tasks and responsibilities. Make sure that the individual you assign has read the box on minutes on page 63 to know how to take effective notes, and is available to type up the minutes after the meeting and send them out to everyone by e-mail.

Whether you are meeting in a small or large group, your discussions can be a catalyst for change. Great things can happen when young people work together.

Greet people as they enter and take a few minutes to answer any questions that they might have. Pass around a sign-up sheet and ask people to write down their names, contact information, availability, and the gifts and skills they can contribute to the team.

DURING THE MEETING

Here are some suggestions for holding an effective meeting:

- Thank everyone for coming. Keep your opening remarks short and to the point. Remember that people will be looking to you for a sense of how they should act, so relax and be yourself.

- Distribute or display your draft agenda, and invite amendments before asking for final approval.

- Discuss the issue. Your first few meetings will address your goals and starting points (see Step 5, page 64) and, after that, you will focus on continuing research and action planning.

- As a group, set specific tasks for individuals to accomplish by the next meeting. Delegate all tasks and make sure everyone knows what their jobs are and when they have to be done.

- Set a firm date, time, and location for the next meeting.

Troubleshooting

Tips for New Facilitators

Translated from Latin, "facilitator" means one who "makes things work." At your meeting, create a comfortable environment in which people can share, explore new ideas, and have fun. Use the following guidelines.

1 Establish a "safe" space of respect.
   - Ask for input on group norms.
   - Manage disputes by trying to find consensus.
2 Guide the discussion.
   - Ask open-ended questions (those that don't result in just yes or no) to encourage debate.
   - Intervene when people go off track and remind them of the central topic.
3 Summarize and clarify.
   - Foster understanding by repeating softly spoken or confusing comments and questions.
   - Summarize discussion into major points to help build consensus.
4 Involve everyone.
   - Choose people who have not spoken over people who have spoken a lot.
   - Ask, "Does anyone who hasn't spoken yet want to say something?"
   - Try a "go-around," in which everybody gets a turn to speak about a certain topic. This lets them know that their contributions are valuable to the discussion.

"The way to achieve a difficult thing was to set it in motion."

— Kate O'Brien
(1897–1974)
Author, journalist

PROFILE Kathryn Kinley: Youth Violence Activist

Some of Kathryn Kinley's greatest accomplishments emerged from one of the most challenging periods of her life. When Kathryn was 16, she was violently assaulted by a group of girls her own age in her small Winnipeg community. Her sense of trust and security were shattered. While she was recovering in hospital, some of her friends found out who was responsible for attacking her and offered to retaliate against the group, but Kathryn refused. She knew that lashing out would not make her feel better or safer. It would only lead to more wounds and leave unanswered the only question that she really had: What had made people her own age want to hurt her, and how could she prevent it from happening to others?

Slowly, Kathryn gathered the courage to take more meaningful action to change the growing culture of violence among youth. She was soon accepted onto Team Youth, a pilot project consisting of a small group of motivated teens who conduct workshops and discussion groups at high schools, with the goal of identifying and finding solutions to the issues surrounding youth violence in Manitoba.

To begin a session, Team Youth facilitators first explain that their purpose is to ensure that every student's voice is heard, then lay out the ground rules to be followed during the workshop, such as the need to show respect for the views of others. In order to put new participants at ease, Team Youth members often share some of their own stories. Discussing her attack was not always easy for Kathryn, but opening up to educate others has helped her to heal and to create something positive from a terrible experience. Combining the insights of students from diverse communities and backgrounds has also resulted in some eye-opening discussions. Working together, participants have been able to identify issues such as racism, poverty, boredom, stereotypes, and a lack of expectations as factors contributing to problems among their age group. Team Youth sees education and awareness as a major part of the solution, along with bringing their concerns to the government.

Kathryn is also a member of the Manitoba Youth Parliament, working to influence provincial policy concerning youth issues. Her activities have given her the satisfaction of tackling the issue at the root, in the hopes that fewer people will have to encounter the pain and fear of violence first-hand. Speaking out about the issue has helped her to regain the confidence that she had lost in the attack, and to transform one of her most difficult experiences into a moment of leadership, growth, and social change.

1 How were the Team Youth meetings helpful to Kathryn and her peers in discovering the root causes of youth violence in their communities?
2 Try to imagine yourself in a position similar to Kathryn's. How could your group make you feel comfortable talking about a difficult experience that relates to your issue? How could they turn it into an empowering experience for both you and the team?
3 Brainstorm a list of group norms or ground rules to make your meetings more effective and encourage everyone (especially quiet people) to participate freely and to share their different perspectives.

RECORDING MINUTES OF THE MEETING

The minutes for your meeting should include the following:

- The name of your group

- The date, time, and place of the meeting

- Who is present

- Who has sent their regrets

- Who is missing

- The agenda for the meeting

- A short summary of what was discussed with respect to each agenda item, and points made by individual members

- Statement of decisions made

- Tasks delegated for next meeting

- Date, time, and place for next meeting and the roles assigned

- Time the meeting was adjourned (ended)

Evaluating what happened at the meeting

Take some time at the end of the meeting to talk about the meeting itself. Ask your Core Group to consider the following questions:

- What went right and what went wrong, and why?

- Did we meet the goals we set for ourselves?

- Did we address all the points on the agenda?

- Was the discussion on track or unfocused?

- Did we make an effort to help everyone feel comfortable and participate?

- Did group members listen effectively and build on one another's ideas?

- Are we all committed to the decisions that we made?

- Does everyone feel empowered to take on his or her responsibilities?

- Did we have fun?

- What should we do differently next time?

You're not off the hook just yet. After the meeting, don't forget to:

- Call or e-mail first-time participants and thank them for coming.

- To all group members, distribute or e-mail a copy of the minutes to remind them of tasks they agreed to complete before the next meeting.

- Follow up with some people individually, especially those who may need encouragement to see their tasks through. Inform the group that you will be checking in with people in case anyone needs any help. Be sure to assess progress on actions during subsequent meetings. Make yourself available.

Take Action!

1 Write a draft agenda for a meeting that you could have on your chosen issue.

2 Brainstorm five great icebreakers and team-building activities, and three potential post-meeting activities you would try at a meeting. Share your list with a group of three or four others. Add the ideas you like to your list.

3 Hold a meeting on your chosen issue. It could be at school or at your home on the weekend. Don't forget the agenda, the minute taker, the food, and the fun!

Step 5: Set a Mission

You are now passionate about an issue that you understand very well. You have a Dream Team, and you are ready to hold effective meetings. It is time, then, to focus on a critical question: What do you want to do? Most of this step will be part of the main discussion at your first few meetings.

In order to turn your dreams into reality, you have to decide what your dreams are. You have to put all of your passion, research, and teamwork into charting a path that you can follow to fulfil your mission.

MISSION POSSIBLE

But what is our mission? Good question! Your **mission** is your ultimate objective. Remember: Your mission does *not* have to be huge. But it *can* be! For example, if your mission is to have recycling in every school in the world, your concrete goal could be to have a recycling program at your school. If your mission is to provide an education to every child in the world, your concrete goal could be to raise enough money to build one school in a developing country. Your mission does not have to be something that your group will do alone — you can be part of a larger movement. But it has to be what you picture your perfect world to be. The key to mission setting is dreaming.

Mission statements

Once you have defined your mission in your mind, clarify it and make it stronger by creating a **mission statement**, also known as your group's mandate. This statement will be an inspirational reminder of the dream that you are all working toward. To be effective, a mission statement must answer these questions: *what* is the nature of your group; *where* you exist; *why* you exist or your purpose; *who* you want to help; and *how* you seek to fulfil your purpose.

For example, the mission statement of a youth organization working on the issue of substance abuse might be:

Safe Choices is a national (where) *youth empowerment network* (what) *dedicated to preventing substance abuse and promoting positive decisions* (why) *among youth* (who) *through education, intervention, and advocacy initiatives* (how).

As a team, write out your mission statement in no more than thirty powerful and uplifting words. Have each member post it where he or she can see it — on the mirror, desktop, or Web site. Read it aloud at the beginning of a meeting to keep you and your team fired up about your issue every day!

GOALS: SCORING ONE AT A TIME

Goal setting teaches you to translate your dreams into incremental steps that lead you steadily to your destination. Your goals then become benchmarks that you can use to measure your progress, and reasons to celebrate the small victories on the road to eventual triumph.

Major Goals

Your next step is to break the mission down into three sets of major goals: awareness raising, fundraising, and political change. As an example, let's look at the mission of ending child labour. That's how we started out!

Awareness-raising major goals include actions and attitudes that you want the general public to adopt once they are informed about the issue.

Fundraising major goals include what you hope to achieve by giving monetary donations to those in need.

Political change major goals include the end result in changed laws and policies achieved through your pressure campaigns aimed at governments and businesses.

Tip

Your mission may be smaller. It may be to put an end to the bullying that occurs regularly at your school. But you don't really want to try to solve the bullying that happens at all the other schools in your community. That's okay! Any change for good is a step in the right direction.

"It may be those who do most, dream most."

— Stephen Leacock
(1869–1944)
Humorist, economist

Goal Chart: Ending Child Labour

Major Goals

Awareness Raising Educate students about the issue of child labour and the perpetuating cycle of poverty	**Fundraising** Provide alternative sources of income for children and families so that children do not have to work, and can go to school	**Political Change** Challenge the Canadian government to increase funding for education projects for children in developing countries

Concrete Goals

Make certain that all members of the team fully understand the issue	Purchase 10 goats and cows for families as alternative sources of income	Create public pressure on the federal government to increase funding
Spread message in your school	Build a school for children in a developing country	Ensure that local MP is aware of the issue

Actions

"Saturday education day" among group members where all research together	Carnival fundraiser	Petition the government to take action on the issue
Speeches in every home-room before December and 50 posters in school	Auction	Meet with local MP

Tip

The How-To Section of this book has information on the skills you will want to put to use here. See the sections on **Getting the Word Out Through the Media, Connecting With People, Working With Money,** and **Plugging Into the Political System** to help you reach these goals.

Concrete Goals

These are some daunting major goals staring at you. What are some ways you can realistically hope to achieve them? Your task now is to set concrete goals with tangible results, to help you reach each of your major goals. After that, you will need to come up with different actions that you can take in your school and community to fulfil those concrete goals. (There are some fun ideas in Step 6!) Depending on the size of your Dream Team, you can tackle several concrete goals at a time. You can also always add new goals, so start with just a few. For examples, check out the goal chart on child labour, above.

Taking the time to formulate your goals may sound tedious, but your critics and supporters will always ask how you know that your group is achieving its goals. When your stated goals as an organization are clear, you will be able to indicate the status of your progress toward them (like those money thermometers people use to track their fundraising efforts). You will know where you have succeeded so far, and what still needs to be done. In this way, goal setting can provide legitimacy for you in the public sphere, as it allows for both you and others to measure your impact.

CREATING YOUR IDENTITY

When deciding how to present your group to the world, the first thing to do is to choose a name for your organization. Avoid choosing a generic name. "Student Action Group" just does not work. Brainstorm with your group to come up with a personalized and original name. A name should not be too long, although you can always use an acronym (a word formed from the initial letters of a series of words). Choose something catchy and different that will stick in people's minds and that they will not tend to confuse with the names of other groups. Some well-known examples are:

- Mothers Against Drunk Driving (MADD)

- Free the Children (FTC)

- Amnesty International

Just as major corporations do, social justice groups need their logos too! Design a logo with lots of colour that embodies your message in some way. If it is eye-catching and creative, people will always recognize it.

As you define your group's mandate, name, and logo, it is important to keep certain key components of this identity consistent, such as words, colours, and visuals, when using different media to raise awareness of your issue. This allows the public to come to associate these elements with your organization, and to make your group more prominent in their minds. This process refers to an important marketing concept known as **branding**. The most important aspect of branding is to associate your organization with a specific cause and a set of core values that people will immediately think of when they come across your publicity.

Successful branding examples among social action groups include:

- Amnesty International's candle logo and letter writing campaigns to free political prisoners

- World Vision's television ads for their child sponsorship program and their 30 Hour Famine

- Free the Children's "children helping children" and school building campaign

In the Getting the Word Out Through the Media section of this book, you will learn more about how to take your branding effort to the public.

Tip

Get down to a list of three or four possible names for your organization and then test them out on your friends to see which ones get the most enthusiasm.

To be effective, a logo must capture the essence of your group's mission. The Free the Children logo (left) shows two children reaching out to one another from across the world. The gender-neutral figure in the Leaders Today logo (right) shows that both males and females can be leaders.

Take Action!

1 Create a powerful mission statement for your chosen issue. Make it inspiring and post it where you can see it every day.

2 Create a goal chart for your chosen issue. Start with the mission and major goals. Be creative when brainstorming concrete goals. Present your chart to a partner for review.

3 Choose a name and design a logo for the social action group that you envision. Present it to two classmates and ask for their feedback.

Step 6: Take Action!

In 1977, a young man from Winnipeg named Terry Fox learned that he had bone cancer and was forced to have his right leg amputated six inches above the knee. While recovering in hospital, Terry was so overcome by the suffering of other cancer patients that he decided to run across Canada to raise money for cancer research. He was determined to do something so that others after him would one day have a cure. After 18 months of training, Terry started his run in St. John's, Newfoundland, on April 12, 1980. It was difficult to attract attention at first, and for a long time, Terry ran alone. He ran 42 kilometres a day through Canada's Atlantic provinces, Québec, and Ontario and, slowly, public enthusiasm for his cause began to grow.

His action raised awareness and a great deal of money for cancer research, and created hope and inspiration for others who suffered from the disease. After 143 days, Terry was forced to stop running because the cancer had spread to his lungs. He died on June 28, 1981, at the age of 22. Terry Fox set the bar on human courage, strength, and heart higher than ever before, and millions of Canadians and others around the world have followed his lead.

Many people reach a certain stage in social involvement and stop. Well-intended and well-informed efforts to make a difference often get wasted because of a lack of *action*. Actions bring your research, teamwork, and planning together in a way that informs the public about your campaign, strengthens

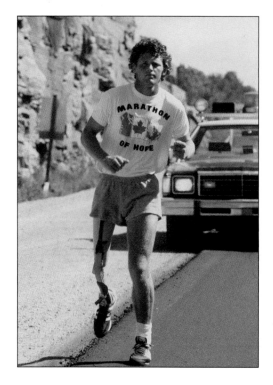

Terry Fox's initial goal was to collect $1 for every person living in Canada, which was about 24 million people at the time. To date, the Terry Fox Run has raised well over $300 million for cancer research.

the voice of your group, and implements concrete change. A well-planned action is a demonstration of your passion and power. It says that you are committed to change and are willing to do more than just talk. Actions are what separate the complainers from the world-changers.

There are lots of crazy ideas out there, and many traditional ones too, for actions that you can take on your own, at school, and in your community to effect real change. Actions can include petitions, letter writing campaigns, fundraisers, demonstrations, presentations, speeches, vigils, workshops, volunteering in your community or overseas, pressure campaigns, civil disobedience, litter pick-ups, concerts, and sitting up in a tree for two years. They can *also* include small actions that your group can pass on to others.

Small actions

- give compliments
- bring litter-free lunches
- buy non-sweatshop clothing
- ride your bike to get to places
- reduce the amount of water you use
- buy rechargeable batteries and bulk groceries
- bring cloth bags on shopping trips
- buy fair trade products
- e-mail greeting cards
- reuse the other side of paper
- buy organic and local food
- do something nice for one person every day

How's that for choice?

When you are so ready to take action that you are about to explode, you need a plan of action! Think back to your goal chart: What actions can you take to fulfil your *concrete* goals? Make sure you relate every action back to a major goal — either awareness raising, fundraising, or a political

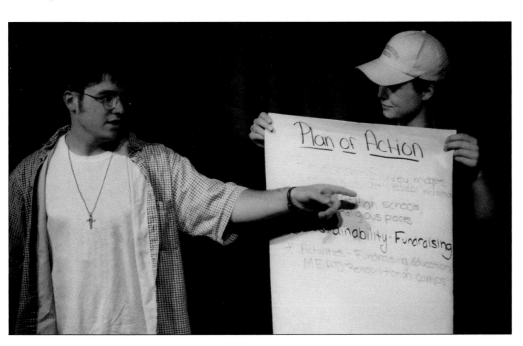

An effective plan of action begins with a sound knowledge of where you are and where you want to go.

Troubleshooting

The Secret to a Successful Action Plan

When making an action plan, start small and get bigger and bigger. When you begin with easy, everyday actions, your group members are instantly empowered. The more you do, the better you feel, until the actions become so big that no one can believe how *huge* your impact has become!

change goal — so that you and your team can see the "big picture" as you work! Some actions may fulfil several goals at the same time!

Two powerful questions to spark your brainstorming are:

- What is a simple, inexpensive way of getting your message across?

- What has *never* been done before?

ACTION IDEAS

You can adapt some of these actions to your issue, while others relate to specific community issues. You can also use this list as a springboard to create your own action ideas for your cause!

1   Invite an activist to speak to your class or school to educate your peers about a common issue of concern.

2   Publish a school newspaper to raise awareness about social issues and to offer a youthful perspective on current events.

3   Arrange a debate at your school between advocates on two sides of a contentious issue, or between political candidates during election time, so they can respond to youth concerns and help your peers become more informed.

4   Take a Vow of Silence for a week. Ask people to sponsor you with pledges for every day that you go without speaking. Donate the money you raise to a charity.

5   Organize a Stand Up for Human Rights Day at your school, during which students literally spend the entire day standing up to show their support for human rights everywhere.

6   Organize a Living Simply Day at your school every October 10th to raise awareness of the social and environmental impacts of our culture of consumerism. Or you can have one every week or month!

7   Start a peer mediation program at your school in which students are trained to act as a neutral third party in student disagreements, to help find solutions that all parties can agree on.

---

8 If your school has a graduation prom, organize a post-dance safe grad party offering fun, alcohol-free and drug-free activities (such as live bands, movies, etc.).

9 Volunteer as a peer tutor to help students who are having academic problems in school.

10 Ask your principal if, once a month, a block of class time can be devoted to cleaning up the school grounds and picking up litter in a local park.

11 If your school does not recycle, ask your principal about installing recycling bins for paper, bottles, and cans. If your school does, organize a recycle and reuse campaign that encourages litter-free lunches!

12 Involve your school or community in a Car-Free Day.

13 Ask your principal to replace junk food in the school cafeteria and vending machines with healthy alternatives.

14 Organize a Global Food Fair at your school that invites students to sample new dishes and learn about other cultures at the same time.

15 Welcome new students to your school. Match newcomers with peer welcome buddies to show them around.

16 If you know of a vacant lot or other outdoor space that is not being used in your community, seek permission to turn it into an organic community garden that your group could upkeep. Consider donating some of the produce to a homeless shelter or food bank.

17 Whether your talent is art or computers, share it by teaching a workshop at a homeless shelter, a middle school, or a seniors' centre.

18 Organize "street runs" to take food, warm clothes, and friendship to the homeless on your city streets and brighten their day. In smaller communities, work with existing community groups that provide these services.

19 Organize a TV-free weekend featuring outdoor activities in your schoolyard or local park. Make it a fundraiser for a local charity.

20 Help alleviate hunger in your community by organizing a Halloween For Hunger campaign to collect non-perishable food items for food banks.

21 Hold a 24-hour hunger strike in which you raise awareness and money through donors and sponsors to help starving children in poor communities around the world.

> "Action is the antidote to despair."
>
> — Joan Baez
> (b. 1941)
> Folksinger, pacifist

A SUCCESSFUL ACTION:

- Reflects the values of your group
- Makes good use of all the diverse gifts and skills available
- Is well planned and researched
- Includes activities that build up team spirit and solidarity
- Is valued and supported by all group members
- Establishes the group's credibility as a knowledgeable, passionate force on the landscape of life (or just as a serious, smart, and determined team)
- Enlarges your membership and base of support

ACTIONS THAT A GROUP SHOULD AVOID

The best way to guard against the wrong path is to choose actions that represent the values of your group and appeal to your collective sense of what is right. Actions that go against the values you are promoting undermine your purpose and credibility. If you are looking for justice, you must be fair; if you want to gain people's respect, you should do so respectfully. Try to ensure that everyone on the team supports the action. If someone in the group disagrees, be sure to consider his or her reasoning and let it weigh into the group's final decision. No action you take should be violent, destructive, or unsafe in any way. Everything you do should contribute toward your ultimate goal: making the world a better place.

EVALUATE YOUR ACTION

Once you have acted, it is important to review and evaluate both the project and your teamwork. Gather for a group debriefing session and ask questions that encourage constructive criticism, so that you can learn from the experience and become more effective activists. To know if you have made a difference, for example, you have to find out the following:

- How many people heard you and your group speak, visited a display, or walked away with a flyer? How many people signed up to join? (This is called "quantitative" or quantity, number-based evaluation.)

- How did people react to the information presented, or to your action? Did you get a lot of community

By starting out with small actions, you may find yourself one day tackling much bigger goals such as building a school in a developing country.

support? (This is called "qualitative" or quality, word-based evaluation.)

- Did the action put pressure on a decision maker? How do you know? What was the person's reaction (in words and actions)?

- Did the action contribute to your goal?

To be able to answer these questions, it is important to *plan ahead*. Before taking your action, set aside some group time to develop **monitoring and evaluation plans** that will allow you to measure your success in quantity and in quality. Monitoring materials to use during your action can include feedback forms, surveys, and tallies. Before a speech, leave sheets of paper on chairs so that audience members can make comments — both positive and constructive. Assign team members or volunteers to be responsible for designing the feedback forms, distributing and collecting them, and compiling the information and evaluating it afterward. A feedback form may look like this:

> *"The future belongs to those who believe in the beauty of their dreams."*
>
> — Eleanor Roosevelt (1884–1952) Diplomat, former First Lady of the United States

Sample Feedback Form

Youth Helping Youth Big Event
FEEDBACK FORM

Thank you for attending our event today. Please take a few moments to provide us with some feedback!

What did you enjoy about this event?

_____

_____

_____

What could be improved next time?

_____

_____

_____

Contact Information (to keep you up-to-date about future events):
Name: _____
Address: _____
Phone #: _____ E-mail: _____
School: _____ Grade: _____

Feel free to elaborate on the reverse side. Please consider writing a short testimonial for our funders and supporters.

Thank you for supporting Youth Helping Youth! See you next time!

PROFILE Schools Taking Action

Check out what students across Canada are doing to take on urgent global issues. Their actions may motivate you to pursue similar initiatives or inspire you to create your own unique approach. How would actions like these work in your school?

Thornhill Secondary School (Thornhill, Ontario)

A group of students founded the Power and Diversity Club to promote cultural understanding among the student body. One of their most exciting actions was organizing a fashion show called "360 Degrees Around the World," featuring music and traditional fashions from Paris, India, Hong Kong, Iran, and Africa. To make this an inclusive and successful event, the club ensured that there was equal participation of students of all cultural backgrounds and body types. For the International Week Against Racism, they designed and distributed T-shirts with positive social messages such as: "There is only one race — the human race" and "Laundry is the only thing that should be separated by colour."

Maidstone High School (Maidstone, Saskatchewan)

Student leaders attended a leadership conference where they learned about the negative impact of globalization on the world's children. Upon returning to their school, they wanted to mobilize the entire student body to take action. The students began by launching a school-wide information campaign. They designed posters and banners with statistics on child labour and sexual exploitation, which were then hung throughout the school. They also organized a Dance For Life event to raise funds for Canadian charities working to provide education to children in developing countries.

St. Joseph-Michael Power High School (Toronto, Ontario)

With a mission to build two primary schools in developing countries, namely, Nicaragua and Sierra Leone, students came up with creative ways to meet their fundraising goals. For three years in a row, they wrote and performed a series of docudramas for friends and parents. The docudramas provided group members with a fun way to educate themselves on important issues such as child labour, prostitution, and war, and allowed audience members to better understand the human side of these problems. The group also organized a Turn Off Your TV Week; students collected pledges for every day that they did not watch television. They have already fully funded the construction of the school in Nicaragua and are organizing a karaoke sleepover night to collect the remaining funding for the school in Sierra Leone.

Halifax Grammar School (Halifax, Nova Scotia)

Students from grades 8 through 12 sought to raise awareness of children's issues by speaking at community events and other local schools. Next, they organized a province-wide youth empowerment conference, inviting students from all over Nova Scotia to learn how to become more effective global citizens by working together to promote change on important social issues. In their own school, the students held a different fundraising event every month, including bake sales, a penny drive, a raffle, lollipop and water sales, grocery bagging, a car wash, and a fundraising benefit concert. The group's dedicated efforts raised over $6000 to help to build a high school in Mulukuku, Nicaragua.

Point Grey Secondary School (Vancouver, British Columbia)

Students founded an organization dedicated to taking action on global issues and supporting charitable organizations working for peace. The group launched one exciting project after the next, beginning with a series of workshops on child labour at local elementary schools, and a documentary film festival to raise awareness of global issues. Next, they held a two-day conference focused on war-affected children, with guest speakers from the Red Cross, and an "amputee for a day" activity, in which participants carried a crutch and could not use a limb, to understand the plight of war-affected children. The group also organized a fundraising Keep the Beat music marathon for an organization called War Child, including a freestyling contest, a drumming circle, a local DJ, and a barbecue. Another creative event included slam poets and Capoeira (Brazilian martial art/dance)!

It is important that you seek out and receive feedback from participants and outside observers, as their opinions and ideas can help you to improve your planning for the future. Also, you can show the testimonials to your sponsors so that they know how well you are doing. In the end, the measure of your success will be your ability to answer these two questions: Is the world a better place because of your action? Do you feel better as a global citizen because of it?

Changing the world is not easy. In fact, it is downright hard. It looks like it might take forever, because it will require a great deal of continual dedication, energy, and effort. However, by starting with small, daily actions and working your way up to bigger campaigns, you can do it! *You can change the world.* Those five golden words sound idealistic. But they are *magic* words, because if you genuinely, wholeheartedly believe them — like Julia Butterfly Hill did, and Nellie McClung did, and Nelson Mandela did, and Mother Teresa did, and Terry Fox did, and the members of Free the Children around the world do believe — they are true. If you do *not* believe them, they are not true. It is as simple as that. *Believe.* That's where a better world begins.

Take Action!

1 Brainstorm ten simple, everyday actions you can take, on your chosen issue or on any other issue, to make a difference. Choose three and commit to doing them, starting today.

2 Come up with one action for each of your *major goals* in the goal chart for your chosen issue: (1) raise awareness, (2) raise funds, and (3) political change. Choose one and describe step by step how you will implement the action — whom will you get to help, where will you start, what materials and preparation will you need?

3 Carry out your one action on your chosen issue. Don't forget to celebrate when you succeed!

Step 7: Bring in the Fun!

The most amazing, fantastic, and electrifying thing about taking action is that, in order to *truly* succeed, you must have *fun*! Without it, you will succumb to despair during those inevitable moments of your campaign when you feel overwhelmed, discouraged, or even bored. This is natural; your dream world will not arrive overnight, spontaneously showing up at your front door one day. Being an active global citizen will often mean taking risks, going against what is popular, and putting yourself on the line. You will encounter opposition along the way. But with the power of fun, your world-changing voyage will become an adventure! Remember: Having fun does not mean that you are not committed to the issue. It means that your dedication fulfils you, makes you feel good about yourself, and motivates you to do more.

When Free the Children was first founded, a radio talk show host in Toronto publicly announced that young people were interested in malls and video games, and that it was abnormal for us to be speaking out about social issues. The only thing youth are interested in is having fun, he said. However, with our determination, our research, our passionate Level 3 spirit, we have proved people like him wrong. We *have* changed the world. And we've also had the time of our lives!

Here's how to set the fun-o-meter on *high*:

- Celebrate your victories, big and small — have a superhero costume party, watch a ball game on TV, or enjoy a big tub of ice cream together.

- Let your meetings build friendships as well as action plans — have a fun break with a team-building exercise like building a human pyramid or a huge shoe tower!

- Let go of your inhibitions and try new, fun ideas that sound crazy at first — the more you can truly be yourself and break away from the confines of "cool," the more people will pay attention!

To stay positive, remember your passion booster — that picture, or ring, or poem you keep handy to remind you of your mission, and rekindle your commitment to act (see page 44). Surround yourself with teammates who inspire and encourage one another. Remind each other why you first became involved, and refuse to compromise the values that brought you together. Make a regular habit out of affirmation, either spontaneously or as part of a meeting. When you hang around with people who believe in you, your belief in yourself will never let you down.

And finally, look to role models to remind you of what is possible. From Louise Arbor and Terry Fox to local activists, your family and teachers, people have overcome huge obstacles to make this world the beautiful place that it is. We have come a long way on the tireless efforts of millions before us. But there is more work to do. Our legacy begins now.

> *"Don't be afraid of opposition. Remember a kite rises against, not with, the wind."*
>
> — Hamilton Mabie (1845–1916) Author, editor, and critic

Celebrate your victories in different and fun ways. These teens got together to form a human pyramid.

Take Action!

1 Think of five ways that you could celebrate an accomplishment that is small, but still deserves to be celebrated.

2 Think of five amazing ways that you could celebrate a major accomplishment.

PROFILE Amber Herman: Substance Abuse Activist

While driving to a friend's house one evening, 17-year-old Amber Herman watched a van speed through an intersection in front of her. Soon the road was blocked by police cars and an ambulance, and Amber was forced to pull over. She realized that the van had hit a telephone pole. The 18-year-old driver had been drunk. Amber stood by helplessly and saw the 11-year-old passenger die. Frightened and shaken, she thought about how easily she or someone she loved could have been hit by the van, and realized how tragic — yet preventable — the consequences of alcohol abuse could be. That night, Amber vowed to turn the experience into something positive by establishing a chapter of a national substance abuse awareness program, Students Against Destructive Decisions (SADD), by the upcoming school year. And she did.

To create a vision for the SADD program at her school, Amber did research on SADD's national Web page and spoke to students involved with SADD programs at other area high schools. Next, she compiled information on SADD from student manuals, recruited members by e-mail, and sought out adult advisors who could provide guidance to the group. Amber's efforts paid off when 40 students showed up for her first meeting, proving that others shared her concerns. Her passion turned out to be contagious, as SADD members brainstormed ideas and put them into action over the next few months through events such as substance-free bonfires and dances, car crash displays, and skits about peer pressure. The SADD group got their message out to the community through public service announcements (PSAs) in the local media and by collaborating in youth preventative programs with local police and fire departments.

Amber focused on making the spirit of SADD uplifting and positive, but her experiences were not always easy. She encountered initial doubts from her school counsellor, who did not believe that a SADD program could succeed in a high school where most students drank. Amber's greatest opposition came from the people she was trying to help: her peers, who did not like having their actions challenged. Most members of SADD lost a few friends, but Amber refused to compromise on her position about the seriousness of teenage substance abuse. Her conviction earned the respect of other students, who began to see her as a role model. Many thanked her for giving them the courage to speak out against the majority and for providing them with an environment where they could safely express their opinions and be supported in their decisions to say "no."

1 Why was establishing a SADD program in her school such a challenge for Amber?

2 What rewards did Amber discover in choosing to stand her ground, despite what others said? What might have been the consequences if she had backed down from her mission?

3 Imagine that you were truly inspired to take a similar action in your school. What kind of reactions would you expect to hear from your friends and class-mates? How would they affect your decision to continue? What would give you the courage to stand your ground?

PART

4

The How-To Guide: The Global Citizen's Toolbox

CONTENTS

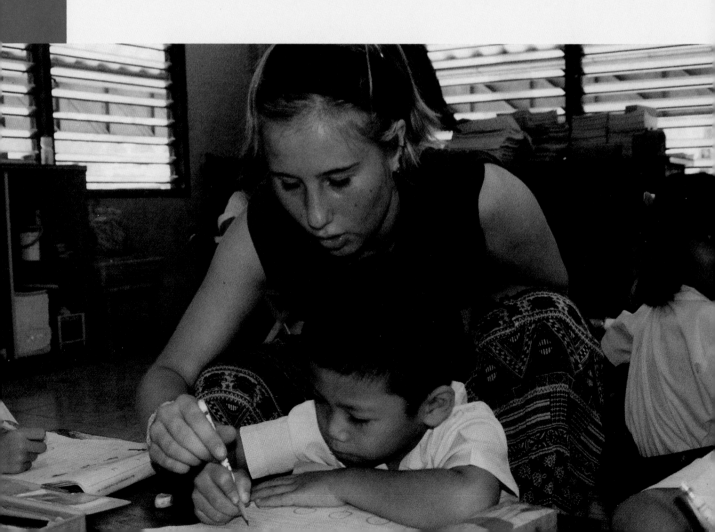

Unlocking Your Toolbox

The tools in that old banged-up toolbox in your basement can fix leaky faucets and build wood cabinets. But The Global Citizen's Toolbox contains the knowledge and skills to fix world hunger and build a stronger community! It is covered with inspirational quotations and images of a better world, and bursting with Level 3 energy. Once you unlock the power within it, you will develop the ability to do the following:

- Cultivate a network of supporters and allies, find creative solutions to conflict between people, and negotiate among different ideas and perspectives

- Make your message convincing and unforgettable, taking it to the larger public through the media, the Internet, artistic expression, and public speaking

- Exercise your right to political participation and work for real political change by interacting with government

- Make direct change by raising money and materials for your projects and people in need

- Assert your power as a consumer by making and encouraging ethical shopping choices on a daily basis

As you explore these different skills and move ahead into new areas of action, remember the values from which your purpose first emerged. Your task is to use the tools within this How-To Guide to articulate your values, to build them into the world as a concrete reality. When used with the Seven Steps to Social Action, these skills will unlock your power to create a better world.

Connecting With People

When you are passionate about a social issue and want to draw more people to your cause, you have to create legitimacy for both your voice and your message. As young people, however, making your presence felt among new networks of people can often be a challenge. Because your words will invite greater scrutiny than those of adults will, you must work even harder to establish credibility for yourself and your issue.

FIRST IMPRESSIONS: NO SECOND CHANCES!

Interpersonal communication begins with your first contact, even before you open your mouth. They say you don't get a second chance to make a first impression, so when meeting people in a setting where you will be able to discuss your issue, follow these tips to make them take a second look and say, "Who is this wonderful, bright young person?"

- Dress appropriately to feel confident about your physical appearance when you are speaking to people in a professional setting.

- If it's culturally appropriate, offer a firm handshake when meeting a new person. Look the person in the eye when you say hello.

- Try to remember people's names. This shows them that they are important to you and that you are interested in learning more about them. An effective memory technique is to repeat the name right away out loud, while nodding and smiling as a way to verify what the person said, or in a sentence like, "Nice to meet you, Maura."

> *"Behold the turtle. He only makes progress when he sticks his neck out."*
>
> — James Bryant Conant (1893–1978) Chemist, diplomat, and academic

- Find a place for your hands that is comfortable *before* you enter a social situation. Try not to cross your arms or put your hands in your pockets. Find out how you feel most comfortable so that you are not worrying about your hands and fidgeting while talking to people.

- Smile, relax, and be yourself. Many people believe that a professional setting requires a reserved attitude, but we say that's *not* what will make them remember you! Put people at ease by showing your human side. That said, remember to address people with respect.

- Encourage people to talk about themselves. Try to get to know the individuals, not only their issues.

ASSERTIVE LISTENING

Although leaders are often thought of as individuals who are skilled at projecting their own ideas, it is also true that good leaders know how to listen. They know that listening is an opportunity to learn and to understand the perspectives and opinions of others. Listening is also a form of *outgoing* communication. Your listening habits can strongly influence the way people feel about themselves, about you, and about the relationship between you. Assertive listening makes the speaker feel valued, respect you, and enjoy your company. The power of your listening skills to make or break your relationship with any person — friends, family, or world-changing colleague — cannot be underestimated.

- When you are listening to someone, take genuine interest in what he or she is saying. You will learn something.

- Avoid distractions by consciously establishing a space where the only people around who matter are you and the speaker. Concentrate on what the speaker is saying.

- Look the speaker in the eyes.

- Nod when you agree with points being made; this lets the speaker know that you are listening.

Even when in a group, listening carefully is crucial so that you can ask appropriate questions and obtain the information you need.

- Keep an open stance (uncross your arms and legs and be comfortable and relaxed) and an open mind.

- Affirm that the speaker's feelings are valid and try to empathize with his or her emotions. Use words such as: "Yes," "Interesting," and "Please continue." Your facial expressions, such as a smile or a look of concern, can reflect your empathy as well.

- Ask open-ended questions (not those that result in just a yes or no) that encourage the individual to continue speaking.

Take Action!

1 Practise your firm handshake with a partner.

2 Brainstorm five powerful questions you can ask someone you have just met. Try them out on a partner and practise listening assertively to the response. Ask one powerful question to someone you meet or run into today, and listen! You will learn something totally new!

3 Choose a day this week to be The Assertive Listener. See if you can just listen all day without speaking (except to validate feelings or ask open-ended questions).

THE ART OF NETWORKING

Your success as a socially involved global citizen can be greatly enhanced by building up a network of supporters who can help you to achieve your goals. To do this effectively, you must identify the talents and resources that will further your cause, and find out who in your community can help you tap into them. Learning how to introduce yourself to people, express your interests, and build relationships that you can draw upon in the future is an essential skill known as **networking**. Making one "contact" can lead to a few more, and from there dozens more, until you have supporters all over the place ready to assist you in fulfilling your mission!

The following tips will help you in a formal atmosphere, such as a school board meeting or a fundraiser, but also in keeping in touch with the new, fascinating people you meet as you continue to explore your issue.

- Before going to an event, mentally prepare a 30-second speech that explains who you are, what you do, and why you are doing it. Your goal is to engage the person you are talking to with your confidence, creativity, and conviction.

- Create a business card containing your contact information and your organization's logo. Carry several of them with you at all times and exchange cards at the end of a conversation. This is your key to establishing contact in the future.

- After the event, make notes on the back of the business cards you have collected: the date and nature of the meeting, the content of your conversation, how that person offered to or could help your cause, and personal notes to remember about the person for future conversations.

- When you have met with someone at an event or a meeting, it is a good idea to follow up with an e-mail to say thanks for the person's time, and to give a reminder of you and your organization.

- Add new contacts to your mailing list to keep them informed of your projects and successes.

- Personalized touches, such as holiday greetings and thank-you notes, are key to maintaining your communication with people who may be able to open doors to other networks, expanding your network in the process.

CONFLICT MEDIATION

When you are involved in social issues, conflicts (with team members and also with people who oppose your ideas) are inevitable. As an effective leader, your goal is to come up with ways to avoid conflicts and also ways to deal with them when they arise. One of the best ways to prevent conflicts is to develop group norms that will serve as your team's ground rules and determine how you work together and interact with other organizations.

Group norms might include such guidelines as the following:

- Be reliable. If you say that you are going to complete a task, do so.

- Be considerate of other people's time. Be punctual when attending meetings.

- Show respect for the ideas and feelings of others.

- Express your needs and feelings, not your frustrations or resentment.

- If you have a conflict with an individual, approach him or her directly. Do not gossip behind the person's back.

When all team members have a say in the development of group norms, they will be more likely to uphold them. Any violations of group norms are offences to the group, not solely to the individual involved. If conflict arises within your group, following are some techniques to help you mediate it.

If YOU are in a conflict

- Be proactive and address the conflict immediately. Letting it build up can create resentment, hurt, and anger.

- Seek clarification by using your assertive listening skills. Show that you want to understand the other individual, and this person will be open to understanding you. Plus, exchanging perspectives can clear up minor misunderstandings before they escalate.

- Voice the other person's position and ask him or her to voice yours to make sure that you both understand each other's view. Make corrections if you feel there is a misunderstanding.

- Express your feelings and needs, using "I-statements" such as "I feel," "I believe," "It is important (to me) that," and "I need" — instead of firing accusations and blame.

- Transfer responsibility by asking if the person has any constructive solutions to the problem that would be mutually beneficial. When both parties are engaged in the problem solving process, a win–win situation can often be achieved.

Tip

Conflicts, if addressed early, can be healthy. They offer a chance to express opposing viewpoints. Provide a regular time during meetings for your group members to air grievances (in a calm, collected manner) before they become problems.

If you are mediating a conflict between OTHERS

When two individuals or groups of people (called "parties") are having a conflict, you can act as a "third-party mediator." You essentially step in and facilitate a discussion or negotiation between the conflicting parties by clarifying the problem, encouraging them to understand each other's perspective, and helping them come to a mutually satisfactory solution. This process often involves asking probing questions to isolate the conflict in terms of what each party *feels* and *needs* (not just what they see or want). As a mediator, your role is to do the following:

- Redefine the conflict from a competition between two sides to a mutual problem that can only be solved co-operatively. Make "winning" include the satisfaction of everyone's needs, not just those of one party.

- Encourage honest and open communication of perspectives and needs in order to identify the true source of the problem.

- Keep the dialogue on track, and keep people engaged.

- Focus on the solution, not the problem. While anger and frustration do need to be communicated and acknowledged, it is not useful to dwell on these emotions.

- Encourage people to come up with solutions on their own that are beneficial to both parties.

- Create a set of ground rules that will ensure that similar problems do not arise in the future.

> *"Shouting has never made me understand anything."*
>
> — Susan Sontag (b. 1933) Author, critic, and filmmaker

PROFILE Dalal Al-Waheidi: Peace Activist

When Dalal Al-Waheidi was 17 and living with her family in the Gaza Strip, she gained acceptance to the Red Cross Nordic United World College in Norway, which brought together students from over 80 countries in the spirit of leadership and solidarity. As she faced the task of representing the Palestinian identity and culture to the international student body, Dalal felt both honoured and anxious. She wondered whether other students would be open-minded enough to see beyond the stereotyped media image of aggressive Palestinian youth and actually listen to her views. When she learned that Israeli students also attended the college, Dalal realized that she would have to deal with her own prejudices as well.

It took Dalal a long time, during her first year at the college, to move beyond her perception of Israeli youth as the "other," or as people to be feared. But as the students slowly began to discover one another, shared meals and social events led to deeper conversations and moments of understanding. These connections were growing at a time when the Palestinian–Israeli peace process was reaching a new moment of crisis. Concerned about their future, Dalal and her fellow students decided that they had to set a positive example for the politicians who could not seem to agree. They had to prove that, despite their differences, Palestinians and Israelis could work together for peace.

Putting this ideal into action, however, was not always easy, and arguments flared up over such basic issues as whether the group's name would be in Arabic or Hebrew. But despite their frustrations, the team members committed themselves to solving problems through open dialogue and respect for everyone's views. As one of their actions, they prepared petitions out of cloth, and asked people in the street to write peace messages. Together, Dalal and an Israeli student presented one of these petitions to the President of the Palestinian Council, Yasser Arafat. They also sent one to Yitzhak Rabin, the Israeli Prime Minister at the time, and to King Hussein of Jordan. The action symbolized the students' commitment to pursuing peaceful partnerships, and challenged their leaders and the rest of the world to do the same.

Dalal had come to see her Israeli friends not in political terms, but as individuals who shared similar interests and laughed at the same jokes that she did. She learned that if they could form relationships based on trust, empathy, and sharing, all Israelis and Palestinians — or both sides of any conflict — could do the same. Dalal had cultivated a new vision of peace, one in which the voices and actions of youth possessed the strength to uplift the spirit of every movement for peace, and to create a more compassionate world.

1 Why did Dalal and her Israeli schoolmates decide to work together on an action plan for peace? What was the message they sought to promote?
2 What would have been the result if Dalal had decided to work with only Palestinian students, and the Israeli students had also formed their own separate group? How effective would their messages have been?
3 What skills are involved in working with individuals who represent the opposing side of a conflict? Why is it important to understand their perspective?

Take Action!

1 Design your own business card based on a group you could start on your chosen issue.

2 Prepare a 30-second speech in which you explain who you are, the issue on which you are working, and why you were moved to take action. Try your speech out on a classmate and see if you can spark interest in supporting the cause.

3 Think back to a time when you had a conflict with another person. How did you handle it? How did it turn out? How would you deal with it differently using the skills outlined in this section?

Getting the Word Out Through the Media

One-on-one contact is key to making a difference, but it's a slow route. The "media" (referring to anyone who works with TV, radio, newspapers, or magazines) often get a bad rap for being biased and sensational, but they hold tremendous power to do a lot of good for your group and your issue. A successful organization's impact is achieved through publicity (news and media coverage of your events) rather than advertising (paid marketing). As such, the media are a valuable resource, a crucial link to free publicity and support for your cause. They get their message across to hundreds, thousands, even millions of people at a time. Instead of just watching the news every night, why not *be* the news?

Working effectively with the media allows you to:

- Spread your message

- Familiarize the public with your group

- Recruit new support (and people, to give time and money)

- Publicize a campaign or event

News does not just happen — you have to make it happen! Your group should have a team of people in charge of media strategy and tasks. Now instead of you having to go out there to the world to make a difference, the media can bring the world to you!

BRANDING YOUR MESSAGE

When using different media to take your message to the public, it is important to keep the central aspects of this message consistent, such as words, colours, and visuals. This is where branding comes into play. It helps your organization stand out in the public eye. Two key components of a successful branding effort include your group's name and logo, which we discussed in Step 5 of the Seven Steps to Social Action. A third key component is your "sound bite."

The Free the Children logo is a bright, easily recognizable symbol. Using it on a large banner will catch the eyes of the public. These children are making the banner more personal.

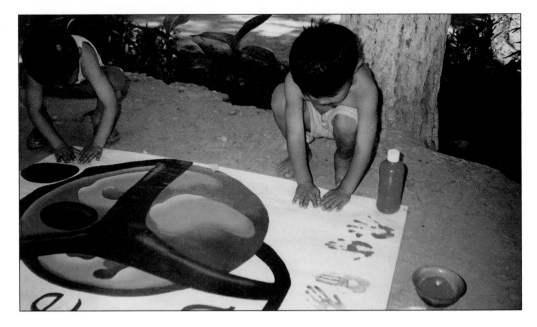

Sound bites

Sound bites are short, catchy sentences or slogans that communicate your message to the public. They give your audience words to associate with your group, your mission, and your values. To really drive your message home, repeat your sound bite often, during speeches, interviews, and when you are networking. You can also include it in posters, flyers, and at the end of letters to the editor, to political officials, and to supporters. Good sound bites are what journalists will insert into news stories. For instance, the Leaders Today slogan is a sound bite: "We are the generation we have been waiting for."

The challenge of creating a sound bite lies in compressing all your detailed information into a single statement; you want to say something that captures your message powerfully in as few words as possible.

The following page contains some examples of effective sound bites for various issues.

How to create an effective sound bite

1 Focus on a key idea. What is the most important thing you want your audience to remember? Try to develop a catchy phrase that will stick in a person's mind. A good sound bite might be a play on words, a catchy slogan, or a short acronym.

2 Write down your sound bite, then say it out loud to see how it sounds. Play around with the sentence structure and the order of the words. Does it flow well? Is it easy to say?

3 Keep it brief, preferably under ten seconds.

4 A sound bite should be simple, clear, precise and easy to understand without any background details.

5 A sound bite should be powerful and quotable.

6 Test your sound bite on a group of students for their reaction.

7 Work on your sound bites before dealing with the media.

Sample Sound Bites

Topic	Sound Bite
Environment	"Water — 2 billion people are dying for it!" — *UNEP World Environment Day 2003 slogan* "Love the world? Show it some affection." — *The Body Shop*
Peace	"Give peace a chance." — *John Lennon*
Globalization	"For every dollar the rich world gives in aid, it takes back two dollars through unfair trade." — *Oxfam's Make Trade Fair Campaign*
HIV/AIDS	"HIV doesn't discriminate...people do." — *Australian National Council on AIDS,* *Australia National AIDS Campaign*
Substance abuse	"Say nothing, do nothing, stop nothing." — *Mothers Against Drunk Driving (MADD)*

Take Action!

1 Sound bites permeate our society. See how many common sayings you can list that have originated as sound bites, and where they came from. They can be from government, business, or social action groups.

2 Create a sound bite for your chosen issue. Test it out on a partner and watch the reaction. Refine it until it is perfect!

WHERE YOUR PUBLICITY EFFORTS BEGIN

Your publicity efforts will start locally on a small scale — at your school or in your community (local TV and radio, weekly local newspapers) — and work their way up to the bigger media outlets like national TV and newspapers. Small-scale efforts require the imaginative use of a variety of media tools such as posters, flyers, pamphlets, and newsletters. You can use them to spread information about your cause and organization, and to publicize any upcoming events. Plus, they are reasonably easy and inexpensive to make.

Colourful, eye-catching posters can potentially reach a large number of people. The downside to this approach, however, is that they may be covered up or go unnoticed on a crowded bulletin board. Banners are even more effective because of their size, although they require a little more planning, materials, and money. The printing companies that print local daily newspapers may be willing to give you banner-size paper for free. Images on banners and posters must communicate your message in a single glance. You want to capture the public's attention, so be creative. Do not forget to include the name of your organization and contact information.

When posters or banners are not appropriate, consider distributing flyers, pamphlets, or newsletters. Their advantage is that they give passersby something to keep as a reminder (i.e., for an upcoming event), while information on a poster may be more easily forgotten. Good places for distribution include high-traffic areas in your school, at extra-curricular activities, in food or entertainment districts, or in mailboxes. You could also get permission to leave a supply of them at the information desks of libraries or community centres. Don't forget to get permission first!

CREATING A MEDIA LIST

First, you will want to make a comprehensive list of the **media outlets** and individual journalists in your community who may be interested in your cause. To start, think about the media that your family and friends tune in to. What do you read or watch? Make a note of these newspapers and programs. Some cities also publish media guides — check if yours has one by contacting the local chamber of commerce or city hall. If you contact other local groups who have a similar cause, or your local Member of Parliament, they may let you borrow their list of media outlets if you convince them that your issue is important.

To get the best coverage, it is important to take advantage of a variety of media outlets and to tailor the information you provide to suit their different interests and needs. Along with the mainstream news outlets, be sure to contact community publications, which

Weighing Your Chances With the Media

Media	The Range of People You Can Reach	Your Probability of Being Covered
Network and cable television news stations	Extensive	Unlikely
Talk and popular radio stations	Fairly extensive	Unlikely
Local daily or weekly newspapers	Fairly extensive	Likely
College or high school newspapers	Limited	Very likely
Neighbourhood newsletters	Limited	Extremely likely
Church or religious news bulletins	Limited	Extremely likely
Community-based Internet sites	Limited	Very likely

are distributed in your area or are related to a specific language or cultural group. You can also check out alternative magazines, which are smaller and independently owned, and are often run by non-profit or arts organizations. Look for the ones that are free in coffee shops and health food stores! These, too, are widely read, and are more likely to cover smaller events and focus on social issues. For each entry on your list, collect the outlet name, contact names, phone and fax numbers, street address, e-mail address, Web site, television channel, format (live, taped, etc.), and deadlines. An organized, detailed list will simplify your future communications. Keep this information in a file or database and update it as necessary.

LET THEM KNOW YOU'RE HERE!

Here are some great ways to communicate your message to the media.

- *News release*: a brief news article that announces your group's upcoming event, fundraiser, or information session, and encourages the media to profile it

- **Public service announcement** (PSA): a short (free) advertisement or commercial broadcast on local radio and television stations, and printed in newspapers, which is used to announce events or to promote your message, for instance, the "Say No To Drugs" campaign

- *Letter to the editor*: a letter written to be published on the editorial page of a newspaper, which is a forum where readers can express their opinions and concerns

- *Op-ed*: an article written for the opinion page, opposite the editorial page. It has the same purpose as a letter to the editor, but can be longer.

Take Action!

1 Draft a list of the various media outlets in your community suitable for your group and your chosen issue.

2 As a class, compile a list of contacts by calling each media outlet and finding out all the necessary information for a comprehensive media list.

3 Brainstorm ways to make your chosen issue newsworthy — what elements of appeal can you use to catch the media's attention?

HOLDING A MEDIA EVENT

When holding fundraising or awareness-raising events, invite the press and get your message out to more people. How do you get them there? Send them a news release with the details of your event. On the day of your event, assign one or two people to be responsible for speaking with journalists. Be sure they are informed, capable, and prepared (meaning that they have practised a lot with mock interviews). Your media liaison person will give journalists **press kits**, show them around, offer them refreshments, and help to arrange interviews. This person helps to control the message that gets out and directs reporters to the most articulate members of your group. When dealing with the media, you want to be polite, assertive, and calm — and not sound urgent or lecturing. It is important to maintain a professional relationship with journalists. See below for some tips on writing an effective news release.

What's in a press kit?

A press kit allows you to provide the media with detailed documentation about your issue and group. However, you do not want to overload them with too much information, so keep the contents within ten pages. Make sure the press kit is attractive and easy to read. Put each one in a folder, with your group's contact information clearly displayed on the front, and hand them out to journalists at the event. Each kit should include:

1 A copy of your news release

2 A copy of the statement to be read by your spokesperson at the event

WRITING AN EFFECTIVE NEWS RELEASE

1 Start with a catchy headline. This is your "hook"!

2 Include the 5 Ws — who, what, where, when, why — and the how of your event and, of course, your sound bite.

3 Write your news release in the neutral third person ("he" or "she," not "I").

4 Fax or e-mail your news release to the media outlet three times. (1) one or two weeks before your event; (2) two or three days before your event; (3) 24 hours before your event. Your news release may be updated if you have any new information.

5 Keep your audience in mind. Who is the audience of the media you are sending your release to? You may have to present your story with a different slant to appeal to different kinds of media.

6 Send a follow-up news release describing the event. Include testimonials from participants about how great the event was. Often, journalists will not have time to come to your event, but if you send photos and details *immediately afterward*, they can still write an article.

Sample News Release

Headline/Title:
Canadian Youth Gather to Debate Globalization

Contact Information:
Stephen Lawson
Global Change-Makers
225 Pinegrove Avenue
St. Catharines, ON L9N 6Y1
Tel: 555-555-5555
Fax: 555-777-8888
slawson@email.com

Date of the News Release:
October 23, 20—

Canadian youth, conscious of their role as global citizens and their right and responsibility in helping to create a more just and sustainable world, will gather together to discuss the pressing realities of an increasingly globalized society, and the role they can play in shaping a better world for all.

On October 26, from 9 A.M. – 3 P.M. at Pierre Trudeau Secondary School (2 Kennedy Road) in St. Catharines, three hundred Canadian young people from as far away as Stratford and London will come together to discuss the challenges and opportunities posed by globalization.

This event aims to give young people a space to think critically about the issues facing humanity in an era of increasing globalization. Several key issues will be examined through a dynamic and interactive series of lectures and workshops. These include: education, war-affected children, poverty, and the girl child. A workshop devoted to leadership skills will encourage youth to take steps to bring about positive change. Each young person involved will also develop an action plan, committing themselves to undertaking concrete actions in their schools and communities.

Global Change-Makers is a national youth action network dedicated to reducing the inequalities of globalization and promoting active global citizenship among young people through education, leadership, and action. This is the first of three globalization conferences it will hold across Ontario this year.

-30-

To make your news release easy to read, keep it neat and use a standardized format that journalists are used to. Keep the length within 1 or 2 pages.

The body of the text should be centred on the page. Use 1-inch margins on both sides.

Opening paragraph(s), in which you clearly state your purpose or main point, and answer the 5 Ws.

Use 2 to 3 short paragraphs to expand on your story using details about your organization, the goal of your event, and any other newsworthy information.

If the news release is more than one page, write "more" at the bottom of each page. Indicate the last page with the following symbol centred on the page: -30-

Tip

For tips on writing and delivering a speech, and answering questions, see the Public Speaking section later in this How-To Guide.

Tip

Before the interview, you might ask the journalist to ask a specific question, or to mention your Web site. It is also common to show visuals, such as photographs, posters, or books, at the end of a broadcast, so bring such items along with you, and give them to the reporter before the interview. Do not be afraid to make requests.

3 A one-page description of your group

4 Contact information for your group, particularly the media officer

5 Brief biographies of the speaker(s) or people of note, such as local politicians or celebrities attending the event

6 Information about the issue: facts and statistics, recent articles or press clippings, letters to the editor with replies, quotations, comments, a list of additional sources, etc.

7 Visuals: graphics, charts, diagrams, maps, photographs

8 Group newsletters or pamphlets

HOLD A NEWS CONFERENCE AT YOUR EVENT

A news conference can be useful if several media outlets want to talk to your spokesperson(s) at one time. It is an opportunity for your group to make announcements or statements at your event, or to launch a new campaign, drive, or fundraiser. You have more control over the information flow in this situation than you would have in an interview. Take advantage of this by being well prepared.

Write a statement (essentially, a speech) that is no longer than two or three typed pages. Have enough copies for all the reporters, to be included with the press kits. Speaking at a news conference can be intimidating, so practise delivering your statement and answering questions.

In the interest of deadlines (newspaper articles for the next day are usually due by 6 p.m., and the evening and

night news articles are due a couple hours ahead of airing), try to schedule your news conference in the morning.

Your location should be practical and easily accessible by the media. You may also want to consider using a novel setting that provides good photo opportunities and creates the kind of background you want to appear in your publicity (for example, environmental groups may choose a wooded area or a location next to a polluting factory). Make sure your location will be able to accommodate lighting and sound equipment.

The usual format of a news conference is to have an announcer introduce your spokesperson(s) before they deliver the statement. Together, the introduction and statement might last about 20 minutes, followed by 10 minutes of questions. When there seem to be no more questions, close the conference and thank the press for attending.

SHOW TIME! INTERVIEWS AT YOUR EVENT OR IN STUDIO

Preparation is an essential part of giving a good interview. Here are some tips to help you feel confident on the day of the event.

Be informed. Do your research and reading from reliable sources, and be able to back up your points with accurate information. Familiarize yourself with both sides of your issue. This allows you to anticipate what kinds of arguments you might come up against and be more prepared to defend your position. Memorize important statistics and their sources in advance.

Establish goals. Make the interview work for you by always bringing the discussion back to your objective —

what you want the audience to hear. Decide beforehand on three important points you want to make and stick to them. One of them should be the what, when, and where of your next event — take advantage of the free publicity! Any question can be turned to bring you back to your objective.

Know your audience. For your message to be understood, you must consider who your target audience is. Watch, read, or listen to various media sources in advance to get an idea of how to tailor your message accordingly. Keep subtle differences in mind; for example, morning and evening programs will attract different audiences.

Understand the interview type. Is it live or recorded? Will they edit it later or include it in its entirety? How long will the interview clip be in the end? The answers to these questions will determine how long your answers should be, whether you can try again if you mess up, and how much emphasis to put on your sound bite.

Practise. Have a friend videotape you while another pretends to be the interviewer and asks potential questions. Then watch the tape carefully for things to improve. Keep practising your sound bite until it's perfect.

Take Action!

1 Write a news release about an event that you could hold in relation to your issue. Show it to two friends and ask if it would convince them to come, if they were journalists.

2 Watch an interview on the TV news and critique the interviewee's style. What did he or she do well? What could the person have done better?

3 Brainstorm a list of possible questions that you could be asked in an interview on your chosen topic. Come up with the answers and practise a mock interview with a partner.

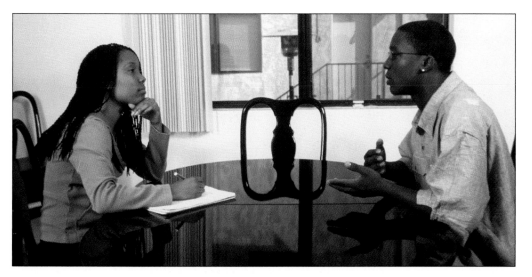

Practising with a partner allows you to hear yourself speak and also to receive feedback on your presentation.

LETTERS TO THE EDITOR: MAKE YOUR OPINION HEARD!

The editorial page is a highly read section of newspapers and magazines that gives the public a forum to express their concerns. Writing a letter to the editor is the easiest and most likely way of making your voice heard. The letter can reach a large number of people and motivate others who may feel the same way about your issue. The editorial page in a magazine is usually found in the first pages, while in a newspaper, it is most often in the last pages.

Tips for letters to the editor

1 Before writing, read examples of the types of letters that are printed to find the guidelines that your letter should follow regarding length, format, and deadlines.

2 Begin your letter by introducing yourself and specifying your purpose in writing.

3 If you are referring to a particular newspaper article, make sure that you cite the date, title, writer, and subject in your letter.

4 You can include your personal side of the story; describe your experiences or those of your group.

5 Suggest solutions — what major decision makers should do, and most importantly, actions that individuals can take to make a difference.

6 Keep your letter simple and the paragraphs short. Don't forget to proofread to eliminate any typos or grammatical errors. Be aware that your letter may be edited or shortened prior to publication.

7 Do not forget to add your complete contact information, including your full name and daytime and evening phone numbers. Sign a letter or a fax by hand.

8 Sending your letter by e-mail allows you to react promptly to a recent article, and timely letters are more likely to be published. Be sure to include your letter in the main body of an e-mail text, not as an attachment, which will not be opened due to viruses.

9 Mark your e-mail, fax, or envelope ATTENTION: The Editor.

10 You may have to send a number of letters before one gets published. Be patient and keep trying!

INTERNET ACTIVISM

The Internet has limitless possibilities for enhancing your outreach activities. Almost everyone can access the Net, whether at home, school, the library, or an Internet café. It is fast, cheap, and wide-reaching, putting local and global contacts at your fingertips. All you need to get started is a computer with Internet access and e-mail software.

Sample Letter to the Editor

It's Time 16-Year-Olds Were Given The Right To Vote

Recently, a special *Studio 2* TVO broadcast examined the issue of globalization with representatives from government, business, unions and the media. A young woman from the audience raised her hand to ask a question.

"Where are you from?" asked host Steve Paikin.

"I'm from B.C.," she replied.

"Did you ever vote for the NDP?" he inquired.

"I'm not old enough to vote," she answered.

"And your question?"

"I was wondering if John Crosbie can comment on what his opinion is on the way in which the WTO has integrated developing nations into the platform of globalizing trade and if the panel could comment on the ramifications that it has had for these countries."

Like this young woman, tens of thousands of intelligent 16- and 17-year-old Canadians, who are deeply interested in issues such as poverty, homelessness, debt reduction, education, and globalization, will be denied the right to have a voice through their vote in the upcoming elections. Section 50 of the Canada Elections Act states that only Canadian citizens who have attained the age of 18 on or before the day of the elections are allowed to vote.

I submit that most individuals at age 16 do have the maturity and intelligence required to vote. Many 16-year-olds have part-time jobs and pay taxes. All pay PST and GST. Should they not also have a say as to how their tax dollars are spent?

Consider how little discussion there has been in this federal election on child poverty, education, and other youth-related issues. Canada was one of the first of 194 countries of the world to ratify the United Nations' Convention on the Rights of the Child that gives children (under the age of 18) the right to participate in finding solutions to issues that affected them and their peers. Empowering 16-year-olds with the vote would open the door to new respect for young people's opinions and an era of equality for all generations.

Lowering the voting age to 16 is not a novel idea. Brazil has recently given the right to vote at all levels of government to 16-year-olds in that country. France, England, and Australia are also contemplating lowering the voting age.

Last month, I attended meetings with world leaders at the State of the World Forum in New York City and talked to the Japanese minister of finance about youth issues during a trip to Japan. On Nov. 27, however, I shall be denied the right to cast my vote for the individual I believe should lead my own country. Why? Because I am 17 years old.

The time has come for Canadians to take a serious look at lowering the voting age to 16.

Excerpts from a letter to the editor by Craig Kielburger, published in The Toronto Star, November 13, 2000.

E-mail

E-mail can be an efficient way to be in contact with the media and supporters of your group. You can take advantage of this medium in several ways:

1 *Mailing list*: E-mail accounts let you put together a mailing list, so you can send a message to hundreds of recipients at once. You should e-mail relevant groups only, however, and do not subscribe individuals to your mailing list without their permission.

2 *E-newsletters*: Send them to friends, journalists, and other people interested in your cause (such as those who may have signed up at an information table). You can also distribute them to e-mail discussion lists and newsgroups on the Internet.

3 *On-line action alert*: This is an urgent e-mail to be passed on through friends and forwards. It can rapidly and easily spread the word about an upcoming event or let others know about an urgent news issue, unfair legislation, etc.

The Volunteer Now Web site was created to help students become socially involved and meet their 40-hour community service requirement. The youth-friendly design of the home page suggests that the site is creative and easy for students to use.

Web sites

A Web site is *the* way to make your group and its issue known. It is easy to access, and if it is done well, it gives your group immeasurable publicity (many social action sites get thousands of hits a day), provides information, and facilitates communication between you and potential supporters. It is a valuable tool if it is designed well and kept up-to-date, which can be a big commitment. Your group should designate someone to take care of this task, and to answer inquiries and messages.

ART AS MEDIA

There is no single way to make your voice heard. The world is filled with avenues for self-expression. While every group needs members who can give great speeches and interviews, a steady supply of imagination and creativity is equally essential. This is where art becomes a valuable tool for communication. Visual arts, street theatre, poetry and prose, and music all have the power to raise awareness, to speak the truth, to move an audience, and to inspire action and change. They can lend a visible, positive presence to your group.

Visual arts

When you reflect on everything you know about your issue, can you envision shaping all your information and feelings into an image? Many social activists express their thoughts and ideals about issues through such works as paintings, sculptures, photographs, and sketches. Community mural projects are also gaining popularity as catalysts for rallying people together. These efforts often serve to beautify vacant lots or reclaim a public space, formally covered with graffiti.

Web Site Tips for Rookies

Tip	Here's How
Make your text Web-friendly.	Convert the text you want to use into **HTML** or **Java**, which are the main languages of the World Wide Web. There are a number of on-line tutorials that can teach you how to do this.
Make your Web site easy to navigate.	Organize the information using headings, highlighting the most important aspects of the site. Subdivide the categories on a menu or sidebar, and include a **site map**.
Make it easy for people to find your Web site.	Register the URL with major search engines, such as Google, Lycos, MSN, and Yahoo. Carefully chosen **metatags** help **search engines** to locate your site in a keyword search. They are HTML tags that supply information about the page but do not appear in its display.
Provide feedback for regular visitors to your site.	An FAQ (Frequently Asked Questions) page can be revised regularly to respond to repeat questions received through e-mail.
Make the information easy to read.	Be sure the writing is edited and polished, and that the text is legible, in terms of colour and size.
Identify your group clearly.	Include your group name, complete contact information, and mission statement or slogan.
Encourage people to visit your Web site often.	Update your site frequently with fresh information, with the most current news displayed on the front page, but maintain the same structure.
Make the Web site attractive and exciting, but ensure the information is easy to access.	Use colourful graphics and pictures. Include videos to download on Media Player or Real Player. Try designing a Flash intro (under 100KB with a skip option). Avoid slowing things down with an excess of visuals, however. Your site should load in under 10 seconds on a 56K modem.

Take Action!

1 Look for a few prominent, reputable e-newsletters on your chosen issue. You can search for these on the Web sites of social justice organizations, and subscribe to them to get regular updates on the issue and new campaigns.

2 Create an on-line action alert for your chosen issue. Send it out to the people on your mailing list (your friends, family, and other interested individuals).

3 Examine some of your favourite Web sites. Which features are most effective? What makes them work well? How could you incorporate similar aspects into your own Web site? Create a home page for a Web site on your chosen issue. Share it with your friends, classmates, and one organization that works on your issue — they may ask to link it to their site!

ACTION IDEAS — VISUAL ARTS

- School can be the ideal place to display a mural. Ask permission from your principal to cover a section of a wall (in the gym or cafeteria, or other high-traffic area) with heavy white paper, and then gather a group to put their ideas about a chosen issue into a series of powerful images.

- You can organize an art exhibit of paintings, drawings, or photographs by individual artists, linked by the common themes of your issue. Place the exhibit in a location where lots of people will see it, like your school hallways, or during events such as pep rallies and fairs.

- Use art and design skills to make all of your posters, banners, and pamphlets more eye-catching and inspiring.

- Make sure to get permission before starting any big visual arts project in your school. Present your principal with a goal, an action plan, and perhaps even a sketch!

Street theatre

Street theatre is untraditional drama that can be performed both inside and outside (in a public park, for example). It is more interactive than a typical play. Because there is no stage, the audience and performers are on the same level.

Street theatre is meant to be available to a broad audience, including those who might not be able to afford the price of a theatre ticket. By presenting larger issues through individual characters, dramatic presentations make complex and distant political issues more personal.

ACTION IDEAS — STREET THEATRE

- Create a funny play or skit to deliver a controversial message in a light-hearted way. Incorporate dance, masks, costumes, songs, or puppetry into your performance.

- Follow your performance with a question-and-answer session, so that the actors and audience can discuss reactions to the play and exchange ideas.

- Hold a "sweatshop fashion show" in your school auditorium. Get the story behind clothing made through exploitative practices: research where it was made, under what conditions, and what wages the workers were paid compared with the retail price of the item. As each model comes out, give the audience the details on the outfit.

Poetry and prose

Writers have always used poetry and prose to express revolutionary ideas, critique society, and challenge conventional thought. Many use their fictional characters and stories to reflect on cultural or historical issues, or to voice an opinion. Think of some of the writing you may have read at school or on your own. Such works as the poem "In Flanders Fields," or the book *Anne Frank: The Diary of a Young Girl* force us to consider the consequences of social issues in emotional, human terms. Stories have the power to draw readers in and help them to relate to people and perspectives that they normally would not connect with in everyday life.

> "A truly good book teaches me better than to read it. I must soon lay it down, and commence living on its hint. What I began by reading, I must finish by acting."
>
> — Henry David Thoreau (1817–1862) Author

ACTION IDEAS — POETRY AND PROSE

- If you identify a voice within your issue that needs to be heard, consider writing a piece from this perspective. Be creative. How would an enslaved child labourer feel about his or her life? How would a stream feel about being polluted?

- If there is a current issue in the news that people at your school are concerned about, gather their thoughts in an anthology or chapbook (i.e., a small, handmade book of poems and stories). You can sell copies of the completed book as a fundraiser.

- Showcase students' creative voices by organizing a poetry, prose, or spoken word performance. Arrange a program of speakers in advance, or use an open-mike format, allowing anyone from the audience to get up and read or perform a piece.

Music

Music has inspired audiences since the beginning of time. It strikes a chord with our beliefs and struggles, and has the power to heal and to move and awaken a crowd. In the 1930s, Billie Holiday's song "Strange Fruit" called attention to the millions of African Americans who had been murdered by lynching in the United States. During the 1960s, popular music became increasingly political, when artists such as Bob Dylan, Bob Marley, and Aretha Franklin sang about civil rights and the importance of social action. John Lennon's "Imagine" inspired a whole generation and beyond to dream of a peaceful future. In the years since then, many bands and musicians have expressed an indignant call for profound political, economic, and social change.

Instead of making a positive statement, however, a lot of mainstream music perpetuates social problems — from drugs and misogyny to racism and violence. You can shift the trend by supporting artists who promote social messages, and, more importantly, by memorizing and sharing the lyrics that really move you. Music has the power to work its way into people's minds, hearts, and souls: the very places where change must begin.

PROFILE Dwayne Lawson Brown: HIV/AIDS Activist

When Dwayne Lawson Brown was 17, one of his friends was diagnosed with HIV. Dwayne's hometown, Washington, D.C., has one of the highest rates of AIDS cases in the United States, with an estimated 2500–3500 infected young people living in the area. Concerned about the lack of awareness surrounding HIV/AIDS among his peers, Dwayne took it upon himself to speak up about the seriousness of the epidemic. He began volunteering as a peer educator with Metro TeenAIDS. This organization provides resources to young people, focusing on HIV/AIDS prevention, education, and treatment. Its mission is to speak to youth "in their own language and in their own space."

Metro TeenAIDS uses a youth-to-youth approach to inform teens about the risks of AIDS in ways that make sense and are relevant to them. It conducts outreach activities in schools, nightclubs, youth centres, shelters, and on the streets. For Dwayne, successful outreach is all about empowering young people by giving them information and choices. Knowing that many youth are not getting the facts they need to protect themselves from HIV/AIDS, Dwayne and Metro TeenAIDS provide them with a place to turn, whether they need information, counselling, health care, or simply an outlet to articulate their concerns.

To capture the attention of youth, Dwayne works to create messages about HIV/AIDS that are compelling, inspiring, and fun. He uses his own creative skills to enhance his outreach activities, which have incorporated theatre, poetry, games, music, and dance. In this spirit, he also created Floetic Fridays, an open-microphone poetry session that allows young people to share their thoughts and opinions in a supportive, open-minded atmosphere. Dwayne has performed a number of his own poetic pieces at the Friday events, and is a strong believer in self-expression as a means to build confidence and spread positive messages.

Dwayne is also a founding member of the New School Activists, a travelling group of "Edutainers" whose goal is to educate youth about HIV/AIDS through theatre. The group has performed at events throughout the United States, including the National Youth Prevention Convention at Princeton University, and the Ryan White AIDS Conference in Denver, Colorado. The New School Activists have been recognized with the National AIDS Action Most Outstanding Outreach Services Award.

Today, 19-year-old Dwayne is employed as a part-time staff member at Metro TeenAIDS, while also studying health education at Howard University. His activities reflect a hope that the battle against HIV/AIDS can be won. By reaching out and taking a stand, Dwayne fights against the silence and ignorance that contribute to the spread of the disease, seeking to give youth the power to lead safe and healthy lives.

1 Why are Dwayne's artistic initiatives effective in raising awareness of HIV/AIDS, particularly among youth? What advantages do artistic media provide?
2 In your opinion, what other difficult issues would benefit from an artistic approach? Why?
3 What other types of media would be useful in getting the message out about HIV/AIDS? List them in order of how powerful they would be.

Take Action!

1 Read a classic novel with a social theme. Ask your teacher for suggestions based on your chosen issue.

2 As a class, organize a competition for the best art project (poster, skit, song, poem, etc.) expressing ideas on a social issue. Display or present the creations in your school and community.

3 Research the lyrics of a socially active musician from another era. Find out what historical or social context inspired the artist and whether the lyrics contain references to any well-known speeches or spiritual texts.

Public Speaking: The Power Tool

Public speaking is a powerful force that can break the silence and raise awareness of difficult issues. Throughout history, speeches have inspired people and rallied them together in challenging times. During the bleakest hours of World War II, for example, Winston Churchill made many speeches that inspired the British not to give up hope. His words helped give people the strength to persevere until the war was over.

On August 28, 1963, Dr. Martin Luther King Jr.'s famed "I Have a Dream" speech, delivered on the steps of the Lincoln Memorial in Washington, D.C., rallied the American Civil Rights Movement and inspired millions to put an end to racial discrimination.

In 1992, 12-year-old Severn Suzuki of British Columbia made a dramatic speech at the beginning of the Rio Earth Summit and energized the entire audience to push forward in the movement to address urgent environmental problems. When you speak with force and expression, you command attention and have the power to move people with your ideas.

MAKING YOUR VOICE HEARD

Everybody has a message to deliver. Everybody has a vision of an ideal world. We are constantly bombarded

Tip

You can use these public speaking skills *anywhere*, in addition to working on your chosen issue; for example:

- School presentations
- Debates (formal or informal)
- Student council elections
- Media, job, and college interviews
- Trying to convince anyone of anything, any time, for any reason!

MAKING AN ORDINARY TOPIC EXTRAORDINARY

No matter what your topic, no matter what your environment, your overall goal when public speaking is to make your listeners *care* about your topic. To do that, you must make your ordinary topic *extraordinary* — something that will turn their heads, something that is so exceptionally critical for them to listen to that they cannot possibly do anything else.

Remember to show your passion, *influencing* your audience to understand that there is a problem, *involving* them by telling them how that problem affects them, and *inspiring* them to take action to solve it!

with messages about a multitude of issues and, as a result, social advocacy is a challenging yet exhilarating activity. As you advocate for the change you would like to see, your passion and conviction must be strong and influential. How will you make your voice heard above all others?

Fear of public speaking is one of the most common phobias in the world. If you feel a little or a lot nervous when speaking up in front a group of people, or to just one important person, you're not alone. There are many simple, proven techniques, however, that you can practise to overcome nervousness and awkwardness and deliver your message with passion and poise.

THE GOALS OF A SPEECH

To write a powerful speech that will inform your audience of an issue and persuade them to take action, use the three I's: Influence, Involve, and Inspire.

1. Influence them

Go to your research for your key information. Organize your facts, statistics, and stories in a logical order to make a solid argument. To convince your audience of your perspective, use a combination of the three main tools of persuasion:

- *Logic*: Appeal to rational thinkers by citing hard facts and statistics.

- *Values*: Overcome logical counter-arguments to your thesis by citing universal values such as equality, freedom of speech, and democracy.

- *Emotion*: This is the most powerful way of moving your audience, as feelings often overcome logic and values. Use stories and personal anecdotes to appeal to your audience's emotions.

2. Involve them

Show your audience how your topic directly relates to their everyday lives. Make the issue personal for them, and explain to them why and how they should get involved.

- Avoid blaming people or using guilt as your primary emotion. Instead, focus more on telling your audience that they can make a positive difference by acting. Use the word "challenge" a lot: "I challenge you to take action." This is more effective

Every speech you give is an opportunity to change the world, even in a small way.

Tip

Don't overuse any of the three persuasion tools, or you may overwhelm your audience with numbers, guilt, or feelings. Find an appropriate balance and you will appeal to every member of the audience in some way.

than saying "You have to," or "You should."

- Do not assume that your audience will know what you want them to do; give them specific actions to take and offer them three different levels of involvement to choose from (easy, medium, and hard), so that everyone can get involved regardless of how influenced they are.

3. Inspire them!

Give your audience hope that change is possible, and motivate them to realize that they can be the ones to bring it about. Find success stories of people who have made a difference with your particular topic, as well as powerful quotations from famous people who share your passion.

THREE LEVELS OF INVOLVEMENT

Easy: something small before you leave the room (signing a petition to improve education around the world, picking up and reading a pamphlet about the issue)

Medium: a significant but easy action to do after you leave, a slight change in daily routine (putting together school supplies for children in need, biking to school or work rather than driving)

Hard: getting fully involved in the issue (fundraising to build a school in a developing country *and* volunteering overseas to construct the school, buying a hybrid car)

WRITING A SPEECH: A SAMPLE STRUCTURE

Now that you are ready to write your speech, here is a sample speech structure you can use for any topic. A speech is divided into an introduction, a body, and a conclusion.

Introduction

- *Casual Intro*: Thank the person who introduced you and the group that invited you, and tell them why you are pleased to be there. Then pause, breathe — and begin.

- *The Hook*: Grab their attention with a startling statistic, fact, or story, or ask them to picture a powerful scenario. You have 10 to15 seconds to convince your audience that your topic is important and that you are worth listening to. If, for example, your speech is on child labour, you might choose an opener like: "Did you know that there are over 250 million child labourers around the world?" The success of an opening "hook" relies not only on the words you choose, but also on an energetic, emotional delivery.

- *Introduce yourself and your topic*: "My name is _____, and I am here to talk to you about _____, an extremely important issue because …"

- *Present your thesis and a preview of your main points*: The **thesis** is the central message of your speech. It is not the *subject* of your speech, but an explicit statement about that subject, often *for* or *against* a specific aspect of the subject. A thesis is the one point that you want to be sure your audience remembers. It should, therefore, be a short, clear sentence, as in: "We must take action now to free children from oppressive child labour." Next, provide an overview of your arguments, in logical order, in one to three sentences: "Child labour is the result of poverty and a lack of political will to do something about it. But there are many things that we can do as a global society to change that, in our everyday actions, and as citizens, consumers, and youth activists."

Body

- *Facts and stats*: Here is where your first "I" comes in — *influence them*. Make your arguments in logical order and appeal to your listeners' values and emotions. Cite facts and statistics that prove your thesis. Describe how the problem started. Explain in detail why the problem is so serious and why society allows it to continue. Make sure to always relate each major argument back to your thesis:

- *Tell a story*: Make sure your story contains several powerful elements such as suspense, sadness, inspiration, humour, or action. Express your personal feelings about the situation and why you are committed and involved. Practise telling your story to friends or mentors and take note of their reactions and advice to make it ultimately effective.

- *List three actions*: The second "I"—*involve them*. For example: "There are three things that you can do to help this situation. I challenge you to try at least one." For each (easy, medium, and hard), explain what to do and how it will make a difference.

Conclusion

- *Summarize your thesis and main points again*: Quickly state your thesis in one sentence, and your main points in one or two sentences.

(continued next page)

- *Summarize three actions*: Summarize in one sentence, as in, "To make a difference, you can do the following," and then restate your easy, medium, and hard actions.

- *Thank-you*: You are not finished yet. Prepare your audience for one last, powerful, inspirational note: "I'd like to thank you for your time, and I will leave you with one final thought …"

- *Inspire them*: The third "I"—Finish with a quotation, your vision of a perfect world, or an inspirational pep talk that will send a tingle throughout your audience. They will remember it as they are taking action and changing the world, just as you said! At Free the Children, we often finish off with "Who Will Help The Children If We Don't!"

- Then sit back and wait for the applause. Can you hear it?

Take Action!

1 For your chosen issue, brainstorm how you will Influence, Involve, and Inspire your audience.

2 Come up with three sample actions that you can ask the audience to take (easy, medium, and hard).

3 Write a speech on your chosen issue. Keep it short for now: three to five minutes.

THE FOUR KEYS TO DELIVERING AN OUTSTANDING SPEECH

There have been many scientific studies done about the impact of a speech on an audience. Audience members are often surveyed after a speech to find out what aspects of it influenced them the most. And, as strange as it may seem, most report that the speaker's appearance or presentation makes a greater impression than his or her words. When you are in front of an audience, how you deliver your speech is often more important than what you say! An influential, involving, and inspiring speech must be delivered with passion and with the following four crucial factors in mind: stance, eye contact, voice, and gestures. Follow these guidelines as you step out before an audience for a delivery that will move them to action.

1. Stance

Stand with your legs shoulder-width apart, knees slightly bent, and your arms at your sides. To avoid fidgeting, pretend that you are holding a pen horizontally in front of you, just below your belly button. Keep your chin up and your nose in line with your belly button (this way, when you pivot to see people on both sides of the room, you move from your waist instead of your neck). This is your *Ready Position*. It may feel uncomfortable because it leaves you open, and therefore vulnerable, to your audience. The more open you are, however, the more approachable, secure, and compelling you will seem as you speak. It also means that your hands are not in your pockets, fiddling with rings or keys, behind your back, or clasped in front.

2. Eye contact

Eye contact is the key to your audience's heart. It is the best way to make your listeners know what you want them to know, and feel what you want them to feel. Direct eye contact builds a rapport between you and individual members of the audience and conveys the feeling "The speaker cares about me." Eye contact also enables you to survey your audience to determine how they are responding to the speech. If you notice that some people have lost interest, you can take steps to adjust your speech to win them back. When you see, on the other hand, that your audience is fully engaged, it will give you a wonderful boost of confidence.

3. Voice

Your voice is what can make your audience want to go out and change the world immediately after your speech. When people hear the passion in your voice, they will become passionate about your issue. Your voice should be articulate and expressive. To be articulate is to pronounce your words clearly, pausing at appropriate moments. To be expressive is to fill your voice with emotion. At all times, it is crucial to speak loud enough for your whole audience to hear you. Most speakers, unfortunately, do not.

4. Gestures

To emphasize certain points in your speech, co-ordinate your words with specific gestures. Follow these simple guidelines:

- Your gestures must be deliberate and visible. Decide ahead of time what specific points you want to emphasize with gestures, and follow through confidently. Again, you will likely feel awkward at first with calculated gestures; however, once you have used them a few times, they will seem very natural to you and to your

"If one is going to change things, one has to make a fuss and catch the eye of the world."

— Elizabeth Janeway
(b. 1913)
Author, critic,
and journalist

Effective Gestures for Public Speaking

Phrase	Gesture
"I…"	Point to yourself
"Speaking to you"	Open hand toward audience
"Three points to share with you"	Hold three fingers up
"Passionate about"	Clench fist
"Come together"	Bring hands together

audience. They are also highly effective in demonstrating your passion and intensity.

- Do not be afraid to let your facial expressions reflect your emotions and passion. Let the feeling flow. Just be careful to avoid exaggeration.

ON NERVOUSNESS

Nervousness is inevitable — even we at Free the Children and Leaders Today, although we've presented hundreds of speeches, get nervous at the start of every speech we give. What will happen if our listeners are not interested? What if the projector breaks down? The key is to channel that nervous energy into passionate energy. If you believe in yourself (giving yourself a pep talk before going on helps!) and in your message, your chances of success are far greater. Little things such as practising your speech in front of a mirror or a friend can help melt away nervousness.

Tips to conquer nervousness

- Know the room and your position: the size of the room, where your visual aids can be set up, whether you will be sitting or standing, behind a lectern or not, with a microphone or without.

- Be familiar with the sound system, i.e., how far your mouth should be from the microphone.

- Know the audience: size, age range, profession, interests, VIPs to mention.

- Know the process: who will introduce you, who will speak before and after you, whether or not there will be questions.

- Set a tone with your first words. A loud, clear, and friendly "Good morning" will give you a moment to collect yourself. Don't forget the casual introduction to set you and your audience at ease.

- Have a glass or bottle of water available. This is quite acceptable in most settings, and invaluable when your mouth runs dry. It can also help remind you to take a breath as you pause to sip.

- Realize that your audience wants you to succeed.

Take Action!

1. Look up the full text of Martin Luther King Jr.'s "I Have a Dream" speech of 1963. Identify the different parts in the speech structure. Count how many times the central message or sound bite is repeated, as well as the number of times King uses the words "I have a dream," and "free." What is the effect?

2. Practise your written speech in front of the mirror at home. Focus on stance, eye contact, use of pauses, and gestures.

3. Say your speech to a partner (or in groups of three or four), first without interruptions. Ask for feedback — first on what was good, then on what can be improved. Next, repeat your speech and have one member of your group stop you whenever he or she has advice.

USING VISUAL AIDS

Visual aids enable the audience to more effectively grasp the message you are trying to convey. Studies by educational researchers suggest that approximately 83% of human learning occurs visually. Use PowerPoint or a similar program to show a slide show of pictures that link directly to your stories. Pictures enable your audience to better visualize what you are talking about and to take away a more vivid attachment to your issue.

Use short video clips, if relevant, to add to the visualization of your stories and diversify your means of communication with your audience.

Creating a great slide show presentation

You can use PowerPoint or a similar program for pictures alone, if you wish, but if you choose to use it for informational purposes, follow these helpful guidelines:

- Start with a title slide in big print.

- Include only one piece of information on each slide. The only text on the slides should be in point form or brief sentences.

- Avoid placing text directly over images, as this makes it difficult to read.

- Use a consistent background or format for every slide.

- Do not use bright or neon colours.

- Do not overdo the slide transitions and animations.

- Use only relevant graphics and pictures, and use them sparingly: not more than two or three per slide.

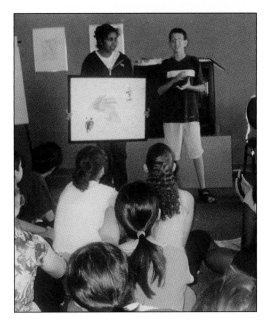

Visual aids do not always have to be high-tech to be effective.

- Focus on content rather than design.

- Go over your speech in its entirety to rehearse the slide changes. Mark them clearly on your speech notes.

- Ensure that you have properly tested the software program, projector, and computer you will be using for your presentation. Be sure all systems and software are compatible.

- Technical difficulties are inevitable. Make sure that you have a backup plan so you can continue smoothly if they arise.

Troubleshooting

Inform people that you will need the lights turned down at a specific time for the presentation. If they are ready, you will avoid having to scramble. Also, if you cannot reach the controls to switch the slides, have a volunteer do it for you. Work out a signal (a nod or eye contact) to indicate when to switch, and ask him or her to be totally focused on you and ready to switch at any time, to make your presentation run smoothly. Do not read from your slides.

QUESTIONS AND ANSWERS

Effectively handling questions and answers can strengthen your overall presentation, giving you extra time to make your case. This is your chance to show you really know your stuff.

TIPS FOR A GREAT Q & A SESSION

1 *Practise answers before the presentation.* Think of the questions that your audience is likely to ask. Outlining and rehearsing your answers ahead of time will add to your self-confidence and credibility.

2 *Repeat the question.* The rest of the audience may not have heard the question, so repeat it for their benefit. Rephrasing the question also ensures that you understood it correctly, and gives you time to consider how to best phrase your answer.

3 *Control the question.* If an audience member asks a difficult or hostile question, do not panic. Acknowledge the question politely and positively, and then offer your point of view. Showing respect will often defuse hostility, and at least maintain your credibility for being open to criticism. If the person continues to be hostile, offer to discuss the issue one-on-one after the presentation.

4 *Admit when you do not know the answer.* Do not make up an answer. Tell the questioner that it is an excellent question and that you will do further research and get back to him or her.

5 *There are no dumb questions.* If someone asks a question that some would consider silly or ignorant, treat it as a normal question and answer it — the person who asked it doesn't think it's silly.

6 *Have questions ready.* If there is a lag in the Q & A session, do not stand there in silence. Have some questions on hand to offer to your audience. You could start with: "A question I often get is …" This will get the ball rolling.

Take Action!

1 Design a PowerPoint or other slide show presentation to go along with the speech on your chosen issue.

2 Brainstorm questions you may be asked in a Q & A session after your speech. Research and practise the answers.

3 Do your entire presentation — speech, visual aids, and Q & A — for the class.

Plugging Into the Political System

Politics play a big part in your everyday life. Public policy affects your schools, hospitals, parks, the funding of your community programs, and the way your country interacts with the rest of the world. Understanding politics and connecting with the government is an important aspect of social action. Adults make up and control the government for the most part, but this does not mean that there is no place for the voices of youth. It is the duty of political leaders to represent the whole population: This includes you. Your active participation is key.

But I don't get to vote! What am I supposed to do? Good question — *lots!* Voting is only one way to become involved with the government. There are a number of other ways to participate in the system and make your opinions count. The first step is to become informed. Do some research on the structure and workings of your federal, provincial, and municipal political systems. Find out who is responsible for which issues and how legislation is passed. Attending public meetings, acting as a representative on a community youth council, volunteering in a political campaign, or helping to register voters at the polls are all ways to be a politically active citizen.

All members of society have a right to communicate with legislators, influence their decisions, and impact the way the government invests in social programs. How do you do this? Through the art of *lobbying*.

WHAT IS LOBBYING?

Lobbying is attempting to influence legislation or political decisions. You may try to convince the government to support your point of view either in person, in writing, or through the media. Lobbying means asking an elected official for *active* support, requesting that he or she do something specific in the interests or on behalf of the people whom he or she was chosen to represent. It can be as easy as meeting with the official to share your passionate concerns for an issue — and don't forget, it's that person's *job* to listen to you!

When to lobby

- The government is considering a Bill that affects your issue, whether to improve the situation or to make it worse, and you want your representative to vote a certain way.

- New legislation could solve a particular problem that you care about, and you want your representative to try to make it happen.

- You wish to gain the government's help with your campaign, either with resources, advice, legislation, or other government action like starting programs to support your issue or persuading other countries' governments to take action on your issue.

WHOM SHOULD I LOBBY?

You can lobby officials from any level of government, from the civil service and Members of Parliament to cabinet ministers and even the Prime Minister. First identify whether your issue is a federal, provincial, or municipal responsibility. In order to find out whom to contact, you will have to determine the responsible

> "The function of democratic leadership, it seems to me, is to respect the past, grasp the present, and enlarge the future."
>
> — Peter C. Newman (b. 1929) Journalist

government ministry, department within that ministry, and, finally, the individual(s) within that department.

The following chart shows how some of the key responsibilities are distributed.

Government Responsibilities

Federal	Provincial	Municipal
Agriculture	Agriculture	By-laws for the municipality
Census and statistics	Education	Garbage collection
Citizenship	Hospitals	Licencing
Criminal law	Immigration	Parks and recreation for the
Environment	Labour and trade unions	municipality
Foreign affairs	Local matters (e.g., highway	Public libraries
Immigration	regulation)	Recycling programs
Indian affairs	Natural resources	Zoning
Military and defence	Provincial property and	
Penitentiaries	civil rights	
Sea coast and inland fisheries	Timber and wood	
Trade and commerce	Trade and commerce	
Transportation		

The Blue Pages section of the phone book lists government departments at all levels (check under House of Commons, Legislature, or City/Town Hall for names, phone numbers, and office addresses of your representatives), or you can research at the library or on the Internet. Ask your teacher or family for the name of your "riding" (federal and provincial) or "ward" (municipal) — that is how you will know which representative is yours.

You do not have to wait for an emergency to touch base with your representatives. You may wish to contact them when you do not know where they stand on an issue, or when you agree with what they are doing. Their office staff keeps track of how many telephone calls and letters they receive on both sides of an issue and then informs the representative what their constituents (the people they represent in their riding, also called a "constituency,") think. Add one "vote" to the side *you* are on! Your voice can make a difference, particularly at the local and provincial level. Remember that because many people choose to remain silent, one voice can be taken to represent many, especially if you can show that others support your position. Get your friends to write in as well, and you'll have a landslide!

Lobbying tips

There are several ways to make contact with political figures. These include letters, petitions, and meetings with legislators. Here are some tips that you can use no matter which lobbying method you choose:

- *Get the title right*: Make sure the official's name is preceded by the proper title. Examples of titles that you may need to use include *The Right Honourable* (for the Prime Minister of Canada), *The Honourable* (for a premier, cabinet ministers, a member of the House of Commons, a senator, or Members of Parliament), *Right Honourable* (for the Governor General of Canada), and *Your Worship* (for mayors).

- *Do your research*: Being well informed enables you to support your arguments with evidence, answer questions, and defend your position. Verify your research sources to ensure that you are providing legislators with accurate, up-to-date information. Know of any laws or bills that relate to your issue and be able to identify other organizations or non-governmental organizations (NGOs) that support your position.

- *Know your legislator*: In order to persuade your legislators of something, you will want to know where they already stand. Read their speeches (check the Parliamentary Web site or read their "householders") to find out what issues they care about and what their ideals are.

The best way? Ask them! Write a letter or set up a meeting to discuss their position on the issues that concern you.

- *Use appropriate language*: Remain courteous and open-minded, even when you disagree with someone. Communicate your message tactfully about controversial or sensitive topics; your goal is to engage the legislator's interest. Avoid being overemotional or making unreasonable demands.

- *Make the issue personal*: Show the human side of your issue by drawing attention to people's stories and experiences. Discuss the consequences of the problem on the people your legislator represents. It can be useful to bring forth a spokesperson who has been personally affected by the issue.

- *Be considerate*: Your representatives are used to being pulled and pushed in every direction. Show that you understand that they are under a lot of pressure, but that this issue is very important to you. They will appreciate the understanding, and will be more likely to take your interests personally.

- *Be confident*: Lobbying can be intimidating, but remind yourself that you have done your research and know your topic well. You have a right to express your opinion, and by speaking out for something you feel strongly about, you may be able to affect politics in ways that will improve the lives of others.

Tip

How do you know what your representative has done recently, or what issues are currently big in your area? Most of them send "householders" (mini-booklets that explain what they have been doing for you!) to every home in their riding. Read up on it, and contact your representative's office with your thoughts.

"Water continually dropping will wear hard rocks hollow."

— Plutarch
(CE 46–c. 119)
Biographer, author

Take Action!

1 Find out who your representatives are in the federal, provincial, and municipal government. Get their contact information and office address. Ask your family to keep their next householder so you can read through it and see what the representatives stand for. See if you can obtain the latest "Hansard" (the minutes of Parliament and Legislatures, organized by day) and look for your representative's latest speech. What was it about? What was his or her position? Discuss the speech in class.

2 Find out which level of government, and which Ministers and legislators you should contact with concerns about your issue. Get their contact information and try to find some of their speeches to get a preview of their position on various issues.

WRITING LETTERS TO GOVERNMENT OFFICIALS

Your first stop to lobbying success is writing a letter to government officials.

- Ask directly about the official's view or stance on the situation. Include a question in your letter that is too specific to be answered in a general form-letter reply.

Think of how much more effective a petition with hundreds of signatures can be compared to one lone voice.

- You may want to follow up your letter with a phone call one week later to make sure it was received. If you do not receive a response within a reasonable amount of time (normally, six to eight weeks), follow up with a phone call or another letter.

- If you are writing to oppose or disagree with something, say so, and explain why. Suggest alternatives or solutions you have explored.

WRITING A PETITION TO THE FEDERAL GOVERNMENT

To be successful, your lobbying efforts must show not only how you feel, but also that others support your point of view. Legislators are more likely to take actions that represent the unified interests of a community of citizens. A petition can be an effective tool for gathering support and proving your strength in numbers. If you wish to petition the federal government, there are specific rules and guidelines that you must follow. Provincial legislatures vary, so check with your MPP (Member of Provincial Parliament) or MLA (Member of the Legislative Assembly).

- A petition to the House of Commons must be submitted orally or to the Clerk of Petitions by your Member of Parliament (MP). Once it is presented, the government will send a response to the MP within 45 days.

- It is recommended that, before collecting signatures, you submit a draft petition to your MP and ask whether he or she would agree to present it (which does not necessarily mean he or she supports it).

- Petitions can be handwritten, printed, typed, or photocopied on letter-sized or legal-sized paper measuring 21.5 cm x 28 cm (8.5" x 11") or 21.5 cm x 35.5 cm (8.5" x 14").

- At the top of your petition, indicate that it is being sent "To the House of Commons" or "To the House of Commons in Parliament Assembled." A petition cannot be directed to an individual.

- The petition should address a single issue for which the Parliament of Canada (i.e., the federal government) is responsible. Explain your issue briefly and include any essential information supporters would have to know. Use respectful, rational language.

- A petition cannot simply state your opinion or complaint; it must contain a clear request — called a **prayer** — or action you want the Parliament to take.

- Do not attach any additional documents to a petition.

- Circulate your petition widely in public areas to collect as many signatures as possible. To be valid, a petition must contain at least 25 signatures and addresses (not including the MP's signature, if he or she decides to support the petition).

- Petitioners' names must be signed as well as printed directly on the sheet. They may give a full home address, or simply a city and province. No additional marks should appear anywhere on the petition pages.

- Signatures can begin on the first page and continue for as many pages as necessary. Each subsequent page of the petition should indicate the topic of the petition. For example, you may write at the top of each page something along the lines of, "Petition asking Parliament to take immediate action to end child poverty in Canada."

> "If enough people think of a thing and work hard enough at it, I guess it's pretty nearly bound to happen, wind and weather permitting."
>
> — Laura Ingalls Wilder (1867–1957) Author

MEETING WITH LEGISLATORS

You can meet with your representative to discuss an issue that you have raised in letters or petitions, or to discuss his or her views on another issue of your choice. Know your goal; you are unlikely to get a commitment to help right away, but make sure that the representative is very clear about what you want, and assure him or her that you will follow up.

Tips for meeting with legislators

- Thank your legislator for taking the time to meet with you.

- Be able to state your case in about five minutes, which should leave time for questions and discussion.

- Bring an information package to leave with your legislator after the meeting.

Sample Petition to the House of Commons

(sum up your issue in a phrase)

**A PETITION REGARDING CHILD POVERTY
TO THE HOUSE OF COMMONS IN PARLIAMENT ASSEMBLED**

(Identify in general who the petitioners are):
We, the undersigned citizens of Canada, *(or residents of the province/ city/town of, etc.)* draw the attention of the House to the following:

THAT *(state the purpose of your petition)* child poverty deprives its victims of their rightful opportunity to develop, learn, and grow in a secure and nurturing environment, and prevents them from achieving their full potential as human beings and citizens, and therefore must be immediately remedied by all means necessary;

THAT *(back up your statement with facts or information)* 1 in 6 Canadian children live below the poverty line and have inadequate access to food, shelter, quality education, and quality of life.

THEREFORE, *(outline the prayer, or the request you are making of the federal government)* your petitioners call upon the Parliament to protect our children by investing federal funds and working with provinces to provide adequate food, health care, and shelter to Canada's poor children, and to raise the capacity of schools in poor areas to educate their students to be equal to that of schools in wealthier areas.

SIGNATURE	PRINTED NAME	ADDRESS
		(full home address, or city and province)
_____	_____	_____
_____	_____	_____
_____	_____	_____
_____	_____	_____
_____	_____	_____
_____	_____	_____
_____	_____	_____
_____	_____	_____
_____	_____	_____
_____	_____	_____

It should include a one- to two-page fact sheet that summarizes your position and your complete contact information, as well as supporting documents, such as three to five newspaper articles.

- Ask the legislator some personal questions, such as how he or she enjoys the job, why he or she got started, and what he or she *really* thinks about different issues. However, do not chat too much if you have the impression that your time with the legislator is limited.

- Even if your legislator does not agree to support you, it is important to end on a positive note, so thank him or her again as you leave. Follow up with a thank-you letter afterward, including any additional information the legislator may have requested, along with the responses to any questions that you were unable to answer during the meeting.

> "We may encounter many defeats but we must not be defeated."
>
> — Maya Angelou (b. 1928) Author, entertainer

PROFILE Jean-Dominic Lévesque-René: Environmental Activist

Jean-Dominic Lévesque-René's battle for a cleaner environment began unexpectedly. In 1994, he was watching television when he felt a bump on the side of his neck. His parents took him to the hospital for tests, and soon discovered that he had non-Hodgkins lymphoma, a form of cancer. Only 10 years old, Jean-Dominic was told that he had a 50% chance of survival and would be in chemotherapy treatment for 49 weeks. Being hooked up to a machine was lonely and strange, but it gave Jean-Dominic time to think. He began to wonder: *How did I get this cancer?*

More than half of the area of Ile-Bizard, the Québec suburb where Jean-Dominic grew up, is covered with golf courses, which use a lot of pesticides to keep the fairways green. After stumbling across a pamphlet linking cancer to pesticide exposure, Jean-Dominic remembered having unexplained nosebleeds and rashes as a child, and noticed that a number of his friends in the cancer ward also came from Ile-Bizard. Jean-Dominic decided that others should know about this frightening connection. He organized a youth demonstration calling for a ban on pesticides and repeatedly brought his request to town hall meetings. He made the news, but when the mayor did not take him seriously, Jean-Dominic did not give up. He could not ignore the evidence he saw around him. He set to work to prove what he believed: The pesticides being used in his community had caused his cancer.

In 1998, he pushed the researchers at his hospital to conduct a study, and their statistics showed that the cancer rate among children in Ile-Bizard was ten times the national rate. Jean-Dominic began organizing letter writing and petition campaigns, and went on to speak to various associations, student groups, and government officials. He widened the scope of his crusade, asking for a pesticide ban not just in Ile-Bizard, but throughout the country as well. Jean-Dominic found it difficult to be patient when change seemed to come so slowly. His persistence paid off, though, when after six years, the town council of Ile-Bizard finally banned pesticides. In 2003, the Minister of the Environment of Québec presented the new provincial pesticide management code. The code, which is also the strongest law in the world concerning health and the environment, bans the non-essential use of pesticides on Québec lawns and public green spaces, including schools and daycare centres. In addition, the government of Québec has decided to use a non-toxic bacteria alternative to chemical insecticide in preventing the West Nile Virus.

Jean-Dominic's dedication has been recognized with multiple awards, including the YTV Terry Fox Award for Environmental Activism and the Canadian Order for Youth. In 2001, he was elected to the Global 500 Youth Environmental Roll of Honour of the United Nations Environmental Program. His crusade was a battle not only for his own life, but also for the health and lives of others, especially children.

1 What were the different lobbying methods in Jean-Domenic's action plan to ban the use of pesticides?
2 To be successful, how would he have had to approach government officials?
3 Think of an issue that concerns you and that you would like to solve through political change. What is the first lobbying action that you would take? How would you keep yourself motivated from one action to the next?

SPEAKING OUT THROUGH YOUR BALLOT

Voting is instrumental to the workings of an effective political system. A democracy cannot be truly and equally representative when people remain silent. Yet, many individuals do not exercise their right to vote. In 2000, a mere 62.8% of eligible voters in Canada cast a ballot in the federal election. This included only 21% of Canadians in their twenties, suggesting that the trend toward voter apathy is not improving with the next generation.

Why are young people not voting? Some feel that political parties and leaders do not address issues that represent their interests and values. They feel that leaders are not speaking to them, that politics are irrelevant to their lives, or that their votes do not count. The truth is, however, that feeling alienated by the political system is not a reason to not vote. In fact, there is all the more reason to vote if you disagree with a decision or policy. Remember, not speaking up makes you a bystander. The people who lead your country and make laws now are shaping the world that you are inheriting, so your input to these leaders is crucial.

Educating yourself about politics at an early age allows you to understand what factors will influence your vote when the time comes. Look at the issues and platforms that affect the ideals and actions of political leaders in order to make an informed decision about which parties and people you want to be handling the issues that matter to you.

> "Progress lies not in enhancing what is, but in advancing toward what will be."
>
> — Kahlil Gibran (1883–1931) Philosophical essayist, novelist, poet, and artist

Take Action!

1 Begin your political participation by writing and then sending a letter to the appropriate legislator (send it to several people if you can!) regarding your chosen issue.

2 Draft a petition according to the guidelines for the level of government that deals with your issue, and invite your family, teachers, and friends to sign.

3 Set up a meeting with a local politician to discuss his or her position on your chosen issue, or any other issue that is important to you.

Working With Money

As global citizens, you will need money to help you help others and to change the world. When taking on an issue, your group will need to base its actions on a solid understanding of the sources of money within your community and how they can be tapped. Successful fundraising efforts can raise not only money, but also awareness of your issue and commitment to the cause. The proceeds from these initiatives can be used to cover the basic operating costs of your group and your world-changing projects and campaigns.

CREATE A FUNDRAISING PLAN

When you are fundraising for a major cause, it is a good idea to stagger your fundraising activities and events. A big project, such as building a school overseas, might take a year of fundraising initiatives. Dividing your goal into three to five different initiatives and spreading them out over the year helps to make each one more manageable, and therefore more successful. Choose at least two major fundraising ideas that will potentially take a good deal of time to plan and will require sponsorship from outside sources, such as a walkathon or a community carnival. Then select at least two to three smaller fundraisers in which you will give people a product or service in return for their donation (for example, a bake sale, car wash, cultural dinner night, chocolate bar sales). Consider ongoing fundraising methods as well, including odd jobs and employment.

Put a different member of your team "in charge" of overseeing the details of each fundraiser — this empowers team members and makes sure everything gets done without overloading one or two people.

For the two major fundraising events, you will probably be asking the same individuals for donations and pledges. To avoid donor fatigue (when people feel overwhelmed by your requests), it is important to leave a considerable amount of time between one major fundraiser and the next. The space of time between them gives you the perfect opportunity to host the few smaller fundraising events that you have selected.

Create a budget

A **budget** is an effective way of organizing your information about sources of funding. It doesn't have to be complicated — some people even get a kick out of it! The following steps and sample budget will help clarify the process.

Step 1: As a group, determine your fundraising goal. If, for example, your concrete goal is to build a school for children in Kenya, you might set your fundraising goal at approximately $7000 to cover the labour, materials, and administration costs needed to organize the construction.

Step 2: Brainstorm possible ways of reaching this fundraising goal. In the sample fundraising plan below, the students selected many different initiatives, ranging in complexity from bake sales to an open-mike poetry night to a walkathon.

SAMPLE YEARLY FUNDRAISING PLAN

September — Bake sale

October — Major: Walkathon!

November — Nothing (planning and debriefing)

December — Holiday greeting card sales

January — Open-mike poetry night

February — Valentine-o-grams sales

March — Spaghetti dinner night at Nisha's house

April — Nothing (gearing up for next month)

May — Major: Community carnival!

June — Bake sale

July — Nothing (taking a break)

August — Car wash

Step 3: Estimate the expenses involved in organizing each of these fundraising initiatives. You may wish to seek the advice of people who have carried out similar campaigns or who are familiar with budgeting for community efforts. As you estimate costs, try to be as detailed and specific as possible. Because raising a lot of money is often a challenge for youth groups, it is a good idea to plan to keep your expenses as low as possible.

As an example, the expenses involved in an initiative such as a walkathon might include the cost of flyers and posters to advertise the event, pledge forms, bottles of water, and town licences to host a post-event party in the park. As you estimate the cost of these items, consider how many of them can be covered by in-kind donations and make a note of organizations and businesses that can support your cause with their contributions. Record all the projected expenses and in-kind donations in your budget, using the sample walkathon budget on page 124 as a model.

Step 4: Estimate the projected revenue from the fundraising initiative (the money you expect to bring in). For a walkathon, you would raise money primarily through sponsorship by students and adults. Estimate roughly how much money participants

Troubleshooting

Keeping the Costs Down

- **Get facilities donated or work out of someone's home.**

- **Get lots of in-kind donations — meaning businesses give away what they make, such as supplies (like food, drinks, or CDs); services (like baseball tickets or mini-golf coupons); or things people aren't using any more (like computers, telephones, or filing cabinets).**

- **Recruit volunteers — remember your Minga Team? This is their time to shine!**

- **Send your newsletters out by e-mail instead of by post.**

- **Research long distance telephone plans for the one that suits your needs most economically.**

- **Find an existing organization on which you can piggyback resources such as mail-outs, telephone calls, office space, media lists, etc.**

are likely to raise. Record the projected revenue in your budget, listing each different source on a separate line.

Step 5: Total each column separately: revenue, in-kind donations, and expenses. Then compare the projected fundraising revenue with the projected expenses. Subtracting the expenses from the revenue will determine the net income of your fundraising initiative

CONTINGENCY FUNDS: JUST IN CASE

Even though you may plan your budget carefully, unforeseen events and circumstances often arise and can result in additional expenses. To compensate for these unexpected costs, it is usually a good idea to factor **contingency funds** into your budget. Contingency funds should be recorded on a separate line in the budget and can be anywhere from 3% to 5% of your total expenses.

Sample Walkathon Budget

BUDGET
Walkathon Fundraiser to Build a School in Kenya
Goal: $7000

Item	Details	Revenue	In-Kind Donation	Expense
Sponsorship by students	330 students x generating, on average, $15 each through sponsorships/pledges	$4950		
Sponsorship by adults	15 teachers x generating, on average, $30 each through sponsorships/pledges	$450		
Promotional materials	Copy expenses for flyers and posters (Donated by Carrie's Copy and Print Centre)		$150	
Pledge forms	Specially designed for computer tracking purposes of income and donors			$220
Transportation	On day of event to set up walk route (gas and mileage expenses)			$30
Telephone	Long distance expenses to call sponsors			$12
Bottles of water	Donated by Spring Water Inc.		$350	
Police fees	Money needed to hire police officer to direct traffic to ensure safety			$360
Licences	Town licence necessary for post-walk party in park			$75
Prizes	Prizes for students with most money collected (Donated by Trophies Inc.)		$60	
Contingency	In case of any unforeseen expenses			$35
TOTALS		**$5400**	**$560**	**$732**

According to the budget, a net income of $4668 would be raised in cash donations, and $560 would be raised through in-kind donations.

and will help you to determine how close it will bring you to your ultimate fundraising goal!

Once the budget is made, distribute detailed copies to your group members and ask for their input. They may think of something you forgot, or have a great idea to get something donated! When individual members feel involved with the goals of the group, they are committed to working toward them.

Take Action!

1 Brainstorm 10 to 20 local businesses that might be willing to make in-kind donations to an event held by a social action group, and what they could contribute.

2 Select one action from the goal chart you developed in the Seven Steps to Social Action section (see page 68). Create a draft budget for that action — what would your expenses be? Put a star next to those items you could get donated in kind. Don't forget the contingency funds!

GREAT FUNDRAISERS

Look through the list in the box below for fundraising ideas that you would like to try. Or be creative and come up with your own! People get excited when something is new and different. A good fundraiser should boost your spirits as well as your budget.

Remember to get permission to hold an event in your school or community before beginning to organize.

FUNDRAISING IDEAS

1 **Raffles**: Request local businesses to donate a variety of items to give away as prizes. Sell tickets and raffle off the items. Each winner receives a prize.

2 **Candy or Card Sales**: Ask businesses to provide merchandise that you can sell, ensuring that at least half of the proceeds go toward your cause. Or, ask an artistic friend to help design a holiday greeting card and have them printed to sell.

3 **Car Wash**: Organize a car wash in the parking lot of your school, place of worship, or public area, and have your group bring supplies from home.

4 **Silent Auction**: Hold a silent auction for donated items, such as a pair of hockey season's tickets or esthetic services.

5 **Guest Speaker**: Invite a guest speaker associated with your cause to your home, school, or community hall and sell tickets to the event.

6 *Bracelets for Freedom*: Make bracelets with colourful thread or beads and sell them for roughly $1 each. They'll go fast!

7 *Tip-A-Teen*: Have your friends volunteer as servers for the day in a deli or a café. Dress up crazy, and liven up the place a little. Ask the deli/café managers if they will donate 10% of the day's profits and tips to your group.

8 *Dump the Change*: Every Friday during the school year, staff and students at your school can dump their small change into a jar. At the end of the semester or school year, the change can be put toward your goal.

9 *Dress Down Day or Dress Glam Day*: Students pay $2 to "dress down" at school or to dress as a celebrity.

10 *World Food Fair*: Sell tickets to a banquet featuring dishes from different parts of the world.

11 *Theme Party or Dance*: Ask students to come to the party dressed as a television character or favourite music star, depending on the theme. Charge admission at the door. People can buy ballots to vote for their favourite costume and, at the end of the evening, the winner receives a prize.

12 *Garage Auction*: Have a garage sale, but sell items auction-style. Bring things from home that you do not want anymore, and have the auction during lunch hour.

13 *Talent Show*: You can twist the idea around so that it will be a talent show involving only movie spoofs, or one in which participants sing well-known songs for which they have changed the lyrics. Be creative!

14 *Match Your Money*: When you have reached your fundraising goal, contact community organizations and business groups and ask them to match the money that you raised. Do not forget to write thank-you notes afterward.

15 *Bazaar*: Sell goods and provide services. Your items can include: barbecued food, cookies, muffins, and artwork. You can also teach people how to make bracelets or other crafts. Again, it is all about creativity and making your market different from other conventional markets. This is the key to attracting more people.

16 *Pop-Can Drive*: Have a contest within your school, including teachers, to collect as many cans as possible. Collect money for the cans from a recycling centre. You decide how long you want the can drive to run.

17 *Request a Share in the Profits*: Pick a popular event in your city or town (sports/theatre/concert), and ask the organizers, far in advance, about sharing the profits. Suggest that they mention their sponsorship of you in the printed program. This way, they receive recognition, and more people become aware of your cause.

18 *Grocery receipts*: Collect grocery store receipts and ask the store to donate a percentage of the total sales listed on the receipts. Make this agreement with the store manager before you start collecting.

19 *Day-Old Donations*: Ask a local coffee shop to donate their "day-old" doughnuts. Sell the doughnuts during lunchtime. This idea works with any kind of donated baked goods — check with a local bakery.

20 *Restaurant Fundraiser*: Ask a restaurant to sponsor a fundraising dinner. They may provide food "at cost" or cover the cost of the entire evening. Sell tickets to the general public. This is a great way for a restaurant to promote itself.

21 *Walkathon*: Invite your community to participate in a walk/run through a park in your area (you can plan how long the route will be). Charge participants a sign-up fee (offer a slightly lower cost per family) and have them ask for sponsors to donate to the cause. Ask a grocery store to donate food for a breakfast/brunch to serve participants afterward.

22 *Benefit performance*: Ask a local entertainer (musician/magician/clown) to donate his or her talents for an evening performance. Ask your local hall to donate the space for the performance. Sell tickets and promote the event well in advance.

23 *Sports Contest*: Organize an arm wrestling contest or a basketball free-throw contest. Have people pay a sign-up fee to participate. Hold it in the gym during lunchtime and announce the winner over the PA system.

24 *Banquet*: Many schools have banquets recognizing student athletes. Ask the organizers to share part of the ticket sales. Offer to help with the organizing of the banquet.

25 *Community Party*: You can hold it at someone's house or in a more public place (try to get the space for free). Ask a local caterer or grocery store to provide the food, either free or "at cost." Set up a volleyball net or soccer goal posts and other games. Sell tickets to the general public well before the event so that you know how much food to have on hand.

26 *Second-Hand Sales*: Find businesses in your area that buy used clothing (called consignment shops) and used CDs. Collect the clothing and CDs to sell. Everyone gets to clean out their closets and contribute to your cause at the same time.

27 *War Is Not a Game*: Organize war toy "trade-ins" in your school to make a symbolic statement that says, "While we play war, for millions of kids around the world, war is not a game." Get sponsors to donate a set amount for each war toy turned in.

28 *Child Labour for Child Labour*: Perform odd jobs around your neighbourhood in return for pledges or donations to help child labourers around the world. These jobs might include neighbourhood beautification projects, lawn mowing, snow shovelling, and window cleaning.

29 *Speeches*: Give a speech about your issue at a community event, place of worship, or local service club, and request donations for your cause.

MAKING THE MOST OF YOUR FUNDRAISING EVENT

Most people do not realize that it is possible to raise money before, during, and after a fundraising event. To make the occasion as productive as possible, consider every moment a valuable fundraising opportunity.

If your fundraiser is a charity softball event, for example, there are many ways, outside of ticket sales, in which you can raise funds. It is important, however, to select only two or three fundraising activities for each time period. Too many gimmicks may appear exploitative and can turn people away from contributing to your cause. The table on the next page provides some ideas.

WHO TO ASK FOR MONEY

Think of all the different groups of people or institutions that can help you fundraise for your project — through pledges, donations, and participation in your events. Start with your family's address book, the Internet, and the telephone directory to draw upon all your potential sources of funding. It is always best to start with individuals, businesses, and other organizations that share similar values and would likely be sympathetic and supportive of your cause. Aside from your friends and family, this list might include the following:

- Adults at school (teachers, guidance counsellors, principal, parent/teacher council)

These young people looked around their homes for things that they no longer needed and organized a yard sale to raise money for their cause. You don't have to look very far to find a way to change the world.

Making the Most of Your Event: Charity Softball

Timing	Fundraising Action
Before	• Find corporate sponsors • Sell tickets to the game • Collect celebrity memorabilia to auction off • Hold a pre-event reception (night or day before) • Organize valet parking
During	• Raffle off the first pitch • Take pictures with celebrities • Offer celebrity autographs • Wash cars during the game • Sell food and drinks (hot dogs, pop, cotton candy, etc.) • Set up a face-painting booth
After	• Hold a post-event reception • Auction off items used by celebrities during the game • Sell tickets to upcoming events • Give a brief presentation about the cause to encourage more donations

- Students at school (classmates, student council members, leadership council, specific teams or clubs)

- People in your community (coaches, neighbours, postal worker, librarians)

- Businesses in your community, especially ones your family deals with

- Local community organizations and service clubs (Rotary Club, Lions Club, Optimists Club, Girl Guides, Scouts, Venturers, YMCA, YWCA)

- Places of worship (church, synagogue, mosque, temple)

- Local government official (who has discretionary funds to grant to groups and organizations)

LOOKING AFTER YOUR MONEY

Looking after money is as important as raising it. As a responsible social action group, you have to keep track of every single dollar that comes in, and every single one that goes out. You may be able to find a local accountant who would be willing to volunteer to show you how to keep your records properly. If not, here are the basics:

- Set up a bank account in the name of your organization. You will be issued a deposit book and cheques, to make sure you keep track of every single transaction in and out.

- Select a treasurer who is talented in math who will be responsible for keeping track of financial transactions and looking after the account.

- Choose signing officers (members who can sign cheques). For security and accountability, a cheque must have two signatures. You may want to have three officers, two of whom must sign each cheque. That way you can still write cheques when one officer is away.

Tip

Keep in mind that it may be hard for some people to donate a lot of money. Tell them that "every little bit counts." This will encourage them to give whatever they can spare, because they know it will make a difference.

- Provide monthly or quarterly reports to members. These do not have to include everything, just an overview of the revenue (what came in) and the expenses (what went out).

HOW TO ASK FOR MONEY: WHAT'S IN IT FOR THEM?

When you are organizing a fundraising effort, it is easy to imagine that your group and the people it serves are the only ones to benefit. There are many reasons, however, why it is in the interests of others to give. Knowing what these interests are will help you appeal to them more effectively, so that both your cause and its supporters can benefit.

Why individuals donate

- They are passionate about the issue.
- They want to help even though they are not socially involved themselves.
- They want to see you succeed.
- Registered charities can issue them a tax receipt (a receipt that they submit with their income tax return that allows them to receive a tax deduction).

Asking in person

Here are some guidelines to follow when meeting people for the first time and asking them for money:

- Introduce yourself with a firm handshake and ask for a minute or two of the person's time. If they are not willing to give you this, they are not going to give you any money.
- Explain the cause that you are working for and why you are passionate about it. Try to relate a short personal story about why this issue is close to your heart.
- State the concrete goal that you are working toward. Show that your goal is worth supporting with money!
- Ask specifically for money. When you do this, you are actually transferring responsibility for the issue from yourself to your potential donor. The amount that you request must equal something specific and concrete. For example: "Would you be willing to donate $10 to the organization in order for us to send a Basic Needs Kit

Troubleshooting

Know the Answers to Tough Questions!

Individuals want to know that their donation is going directly to a cause and is being spent wisely. To illustrate that you are competent and professional, be able to provide accurate answers to technical and financial questions regarding your campaign and group:

- If you are raising money on behalf of an organization (a food bank, a charity), can they issue a tax receipt? What is involved in that process? Do they have brochures, posters, or other materials to help you with your efforts?

- How much of the donor's money will go toward administrative expenses and fundraising? How much will directly benefit people in need?

- Who else is supporting the campaign (i.e., affiliations with other organizations, other community supporters, corporate sponsors, places of worship)?

- How will you follow up (for example, if people have donated to the building of a school in a developing country, you can send each person a picture of the school and the students once it is built)?

to a child in Sierra Leone?" Examples of phrases that you can use to ask for financial support include:

— "We are asking 100 people to donate $10 each toward this project. Would you be willing to participate in this way?"

— "Would you be in a position to support our cause?"

• Thank your donors for their time and tell them that you will follow up with an update about their donation. At this time, it may be appropriate to ask for their business card and to give them yours, if you have one.

ASKING BUSINESSES FOR MONEY: THE ART OF PARTNERSHIPS

Most businesses, even small, local ones, have budgets set aside for donations to local charities. They often feel that it is in their interests to donate to good causes.

Why businesses donate

• It improves their public image as a "good corporate citizen."

• It creates loyalty among their consumers.

• In-kind donations give them a chance to show people how fantastic their products are.

• It strengthens the community from which both their employees and customers come.

• They can obtain a tax receipt if you are working with a registered charitable organization.

But it's not so easy! Making partnerships with businesses (especially large corporations) must be handled professionally and cautiously. Money rarely comes without conditions attached; there is often a *lot* of paperwork and other requirements that you must fulfil!

Dealing with businesses effectively:

• When considering companies for financial support, make sure that the organizations from which you accept money are ones with which you would be proud to be associated. After all, you are promoting them by having them as a partner! For example, if the mission of your group were to eliminate sweatshop labour, asking for the support of a company that is known for its exploitative labour practices would compromise the integrity of your work.

• On the flip side, finding a company that actively demonstrates that it takes its corporate responsibility seriously through ethical practices (environmentally sound, fair wages for its workers, organic food growing, for example) is a jackpot! Tell them you know of their high ethical standards, and that you respect them enough to give them the privilege of being your corporate partner! They

Tip

Avoid canvassing door-to-door! There are tons of better, *safer*, and more effective fundraising ideas.

Sometimes a business will support a cause by donating supplies "at cost" or free. As a relationship develops, the business may donate money instead.

will respect you in return for having done your research and being so dedicated to your principles.

- Make initial contact with your chosen company for details about whom your funding request should be directed to, and then personally address the letter so that it is an *individual*, and not a division of a company, who receives it.

- As it may take time for larger companies to process funding requests, be sure to ask for donations early, even six months in advance. Follow up no later than one week after sending out your letter, either in person or by telephone.

- Be prepared to provide the representative with specific information about your group, its goals, needs, and other sources of support. Offering to make a powerful multimedia presentation to the organization is an effective way to secure donations.

- Businesses and corporations can provide either monetary or in-kind donations for a specific event or to help cover your group's administrative costs. When requesting a moderate amount of money, such as $500, you can turn to small independent businesses or local branches of large corporations. When requesting larger donations, such as $5000, contact the corporation's head office, either directly or through the local branch, to make your funding proposal.

WRITING A FUNDRAISING LETTER

Writing a fundraising letter is a good way of informing local businesses about your group and its mission and how their contributions might be helpful. To be successful, a funding letter must follow a specific format, as shown on the next page.

WORKING WITH FOUNDATIONS

Picture a group of people who work long, hard hours every day to raise a lot of money — to give to *you* (and other worthy organizations)! Welcome to the Foundation, friends. There are hundreds of foundations — some of which are off-shoots of large corporations or run by wealthy families — whose sole objective is to find worthy social action groups and charities to support financially.

Most foundations have "niches" — specific types of projects or groups or issues to which they donate. There are big ones and little ones, and a number of excellent guidebooks (the Canadian Centre for Philanthropy puts out a great one) to figure out which foundations are for *you*! As with companies,

Troubleshooting

Can't or Won't Give Money?

What do you do if people tell you that they are not interested in donating money to your cause? The truth is that some people are more likely to give if you ask them for something other than money. When you encounter people who hesitate to give you money, suggest other ways in which they can be involved:

- Ask a business owner to put up one of your posters in his or her window.

- Request in-kind donations.

- Ask people to volunteer their time and/or expertise.

When individuals take action on an issue, no matter how small the action is, they begin to feel as though they are involved, and will quite possibly continue to play that role and move on to higher levels of commitment.

Sample Fundraising Letter

Noel McCarthy
St. Andrew's College School
450 Main Street
Waverley, NS B9L 6K6
(535) 555-4747

March 19, 20-

Ms. Anita Cormier
Fitness World
62 Oakfield Drive
Halifax, NS B8K 9L7

Dear Ms. Cormier,

Greetings! My name is Noel McCarthy and I am the Fundraising Co-ordinator for Kids for a Cure. We are a youth organization whose mission is to help raise awareness of Breast Cancer and donate money for research. As you may know, there are 1 million new cases of breast cancer annually. Last year, our group succeeded in raising over $5000 for the Canadian Cancer Society through a series of fundraising initiatives.

This year, we are organizing a fundraising Aerobathon on April 30 from 11 a.m. to 3 p.m., in which 250 students from St. Andrew's College School will be participating. We are seeking the support of Fitness World to donate a six-month membership to its facilities as a raffle prize for this event.

We would be happy to highlight the name and logo of Fitness World on all the promotional material for the event, as well as offer your company a public vote of thanks for its support during the opening ceremonies of the Aerobathon.

We are also looking for sporting goods to be donated as raffle prizes. If you know of any companies that might be interested in supporting our initiative, please contact me. All the proceeds from this event will go to support the Canadian Cancer Society.

Thank you in advance for your time and consideration. If you have any questions, please do not hesitate to contact me. I look forward to hearing from you soon.

Yours Sincerely,

Noel McCarthy
Fundraising Co-ordinator
Kids for a Cure
St. Andrew's College School

Your full mailing address

Date

Full mailing address of your contact

Salutation, with the name of your contact

Introduction: State who you are, information about your group and its mission, highlight previous accomplishments and successes of your group.

An explanation of the project/event you are planning (who, what, where, when, why), and the type of donation you are seeking.

The type of recognition that the donor can expect to receive from your organization (i.e. advertising, tax receipts, etc.).

A mention of other donations that you may require. The representative may have contacts with other businesses that can provide additional goods and services.

A statement of thanks for the person's time and attention.

Closing: Do not forget your name, your position in your organization, and of course, your signature!

make sure the ethical practices of foundations you approach for partnerships are in line with your group's values and ethics. Research the foundation thoroughly to find out its mission, vision, and goals in order to determine if your project fits within its mandate. When you find one that is compatible with your group, inquire about the application process and specific guidelines for submitting project and grant proposals. Every foundation has a different procedure. Grants can be difficult to come by, so do not expect them to be your main source of funding. However, it may be worth trying, because one niche for foundations is youth-based initiatives.

PROFILE The Toskan Foundation: Working With Youth

When they established MAC Cosmetics in 1985, Julie Toskan-Casale, Victor Casale, and Frank Toskan knew that there would be more to their mission than selling make-up. During the company's first years, AIDS was emerging as a reality that no company wanted to discuss or link in any way to their brand. However, the makers of MAC challenged this trend by creating a special lipstick colour and donating all the proceeds from its sale to an HIV/AIDS fund. They then encouraged their employees to go out into the community and choose a grassroots organization working on this issue to support financially. For Julie, the success of this fundraising effort was the most fulfilling aspect of her experience with MAC. When they finally sold the company, she wondered what she could do with her time and resources that would be as rewarding.

The Toskan Foundation was thus created in 2000, with the goal of supporting community-based grassroots organizations that reach out to at-risk people and provide them with immediate relief and long-term stability. Julie knew, however, that she did not want to simply sit behind a desk and write out cheques. Rather, she wanted to go beyond financial solutions by actively encouraging people to become aware of social problems and to decide for themselves where resources were most needed — and this type of learning, she believed, must begin at an early age.

The Toskan Foundation soon launched the Youth and Philanthropy Initiative (YPI). This program provides high school students who have participated in a Leaders Today leadership training program with a real experience in philanthropy. Students learn the skills to assess community needs, seek out organizations that are working to meet them, and finally make a recommendation for funding one in particular. Student representatives from various high schools select a local community-based organization helping those in need, research and volunteer with the organization, and then give a presentation about their chosen organization before a panel of their peers and community representatives. After viewing the students' presentations, a decision is made by the panel as to which registered charity will be awarded one of several donations of $5000, provided by the Toskan Foundation.

Through the YPI, students learn a valuable lesson in social action: Passion and credibility are two sides of the same coin. The Toskan Foundation hopes that the students will develop an interest in the future of the community, searching out areas of need in the world around them and working hard to make a difference.

1 What is the Toskan Foundation's reasoning for wanting to support youth initiatives?
2 Imagine that you are the director of a foundation. What criteria would a social action group have to fulfil in order to receive a grant from you? What information regarding their mission, goals, and actions would you first have to consider? Write a paragraph describing the ideal candidate for a grant.

APPRECIATING YOUR DONORS

Always show gratitude for the support you receive, no matter how large or small, and be sure to properly recognize and thank the donor. Letters or thank-you cards work best, because they are something that can be kept by the recipient to remember you the next time. Try a simple telephone call as well — it will be appreciated and make it more likely that the person or organization will support you again! This is an important part of building a sustainable organization and relationship. Make sure that asking for money is not the only reason you ever contact your donors.

Encourage a sense of belonging, membership, or connection to the cause by providing supporters with updates on your achievements and project plans. Invite them to your group's events, send them holiday greeting cards, and add their names to your mailing list (with their permission). Regular communication with past donors creates relationships, which is crucial to long-term funding, for a single reason: People like to give money to people they know.

Take Action!

1 Brainstorm ten fundraiser ideas that would work at your school or in your community.

2 Select one fundraiser and list all the steps you would need to make it a reality. What materials would you need? How many volunteers? Whose permission should you seek? When and where would it be held?

3 Convince a partner to give you a donation for your chosen issue. Next, convince one of your teachers to donate money to your issue (let him or her know in advance that this is a simulation).

Voting With Your Choices: Ethical and Sustainable Consumption

Have you ever voted? If your answer is no, you are wrong! Unless you have never bought anything or eaten anything or worn any clothes, you *have* voted — with your choices. Our friend Simon Moll, a young environmental activist, says that our wallets are like election ballots in our pockets, because every time we buy something, we vote for that product over its alternatives. Different companies manufacturing the same product can have a vastly different impact on workers, communities, and the environment. This means that when you choose to support one company over another by purchasing its products, you are contributing to a certain type of impact. Your every purchase, then, is like a vote, and has the power to elect the businesses and practices that run the corporate world.

As a young person, your vote is even more potent. Teens and youth are the fastest-growing consumer demographic. Marketing companies target you specifically for brand names and designer products. What matters to you and how you spend your money is thus of vital interest to them; their survival depends on it. This is your key source of power. You can choose to send the corporate world a message by modelling your consumer actions on your values. When you make informed and deliberate decisions about which companies and practices your dollars support, you have the ability to effect great change — this change is what we call your **ecological footprint**. How big or how small, and what shape of a footprint you leave, is up to you. What kind of world have you voted for today?

CONSUMING WITH A CONSCIENCE

Some of the most important and influential choices we make every day have to do with our consumption of resources (water, energy, food, air, and wood) and products (clothes, books, hairspray, etc.) During the course of a single day, we consume a lot of stuff! We all *have* to consume — there is no question about that. But most of us *consume without thinking*! That means consuming without asking a number of important questions that allow us to assess the impact that our consumption has on other people and the planet.

Questioning your consuming

- Do I need this?

- Do I have enough of them already, or is there something similar I can reuse or repair?

- Is there an alternative that is reusable, more recyclable, or uses less packaging?

- Do I know where this resource or product comes from?

- Do I know who harvested or made it and how much workers got paid for their work?

- Do I know where it goes when I have finished with it?

Sustainable consumption means meeting your needs with minimal negative social and environmental impact while maximizing positive impact.

When we consume anything in public, we implicitly endorse its consumption to others. Professional athletes and other celebrities are paid millions of dollars to endorse certain products, but we actually *pay* to promote them. They say, "You are what you eat." Well, we say, "What you consume reflects who you are and what you believe in." Does the logo across your chest reflect the values you hold dear as a global citizen? What message are you telling the world when you eat what you eat or drink what you drink? How we live is what we tell the world we believe in. What is the message *you* give through your consumption?

SHOP LIKE YOU MEAN IT

In order to compel corporations to act responsibly, you have to be a communicative consumer — let them know that you are paying attention. It may seem at first that one letter can never influence a major corporation, but never underestimate the power of the pen (or keyboard!). Because most consumers remain silent about the company labour practices used in the production of goods that they purchase, when one voice speaks up, it sounds like a roar. Did you know, for instance, that Wal-Mart will consider a change in policy upon receiving as few as 20 letters from its 70 million customers? If you are concerned about a company's practices, send them a letter detailing the specific issue involved and requesting a socially responsible change in policy.

Writing to companies

- Request copies of the mission statements and codes of conduct followed by the company, its subsidiaries, and all of its subcontractors. You can find the company's address on the packaging material.

- Ask for assurances that exploitative practices are not used in the production of the company's goods, and that widely respected international teams or human rights groups can freely visit their factories and workshops at any time. Tell them that you are not assuming that their practices are unethical, but rather, that as a global citizen and ethical shopper, you will buy from companies that best satisfy your request for proof that their products are made ethically.

- If you are writing to companies whose products you personally use, submit receipts to them, a bit of packaging material, or even cut-off labels that clearly identify the product's name. This shows that you have, in fact, purchased these items and will only continue to do so when

> "Feeling that morality has nothing to do with the way you use the resources of the world is an idea that can't persist much longer. If it does, then we won't."
>
> — Barbara Kingsolver (b. 1955) Author

Troubleshooting

Don't Get Sued!

The wording of your letter — especially when copied to newspapers and watchdog groups — is extremely important. You can be sued for slander (oral) or libel (written) if you are perceived to be defaming the company (damaging their image through your accusations). Remember — you should not accuse it of anything — you are simply concerned because you have not received satisfactory proof that its practices are in line with your personal values. Have a teacher or family member look over your letters before sending, to make sure!

you are confident that they were made through ethical means. Mention that many other people share your views, especially young people, and will support only those companies that act ethically. You can do this individually or collect these items at school and submit them to the company as a group project. Ask the same questions about the products that you may be selling at your own part-time job.

You can look for information about companies and their reputations on the Internet. There are a number of organizations that are dedicated to this work and publish guides or Web sites on socially conscious shopping.

Once you are fully informed, make a concerted effort to buy from environmentally and socially responsible companies. This is perhaps your most challenging task: to change your own personal shopping habits and preferences to bring them into line with your values and new knowledge. But believe us — when you wear your ethics, you *always* look good!

BE A ROLE MODEL AND MAKE YOUR PASSION CONTAGIOUS!

Inspire others to be socially conscious consumers, supporting only responsible companies with their dollars. The *best* way to do that is to be loud and proud that you are an ethical consumer!

Live your message

- *Spread the word*: Tell your friends and your family about the new product choices you have made and the reasons for your decision.

- *Encourage ethical investing*: Encourage any family members or other people you know who have stocks or mutual fund portfolios to find out what companies they support and then do some research into their practices. Making ethical investment choices is a *direct* way of voting for the world you want to see.

- *Wear your message*: Put away those logos and break out the positive! There are plenty of clothes with inspiring social messages on them. Why not design your own and sell them to support your cause?

- *Make a statement*: Give a speech in a class or organize a display about the power consumers have to shape a better world.

No matter what you do to live your message and change the world — whether it's doing your research, starting a social action group, meeting with your MP, or making ethical shopping choices, do it because you *want* to. Making any choices because you feel bad or guilty will make you resent your action, and eventually make you sad and no longer psyched to change the world. Be positive and others will follow!

"NO SWEAT" CAMPAIGN

Most high schools purchase sports equipment and uniforms for students, sports teams, and bands in bulk. The mission of a "No Sweat" campaign is to help end abusive workplace conditions of workers at brand-name companies, beginning with those that supply your school. Your goal is to raise awareness of sweatshop abuses and to convince your school or school board to adopt a No Sweat Purchasing Policy. Here are some steps you can take to urge your school to go No Sweat:

- Check the labels to find out which companies make the clothing and sports equipment used in your school and where these items are manufactured. Determine who is responsible for school purchasing decisions, and whom you will need to convince to adopt a No Sweat Policy. Ask coaches and administrators for information.

- Start a petition urging your school and your school board to adopt a No Sweat Purchasing Policy. Hold a school-wide vote on the policy and share the results with the school board and local media.

- Ask teachers to incorporate sweatshop issues into a classroom discussion and to urge their union to support the campaign or help you set up meetings with sympathetic trustees.

> "I skate to where the puck is going to be, not to where it has been."
>
> —Wayne Gretzky
> (b. 1961)
> Professional hockey player

Take Action!

1 Create a flow chart of five major products that you use every day, showing their origins from raw materials to production to distribution, their costs, selling prices, and where they go when you are done with them. For each step, estimate the ecological footprint.

2 Think of a brand-name product worn or used by a lot of the students at your school. Research the practices of that company. Bring your research to the company's attention in a letter, and request information on their labour practices.

3 What are some of the things that you can change about your own consumer habits to make the world a better place? Now get started!

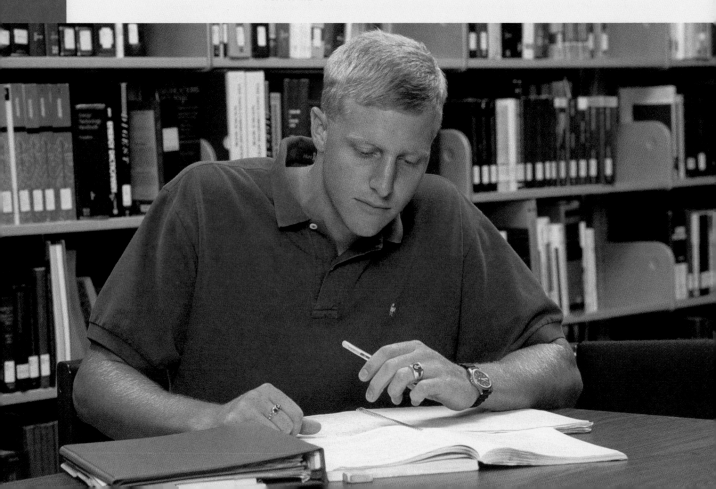

PART 5

5

Sources and Resources

CONTENTS

Globalization/Poverty

Substance Abuse

Peace and Democracy

Child Poverty in Canada

Youth Violence and Crime

Sustainable Consumption and the Environment

Racism

Exploitation of Children

Aboriginal Rights

HIV/AIDS

Check out the following organizations that are working on a wide range of global issues. Many of these are youth organizations, started by and for young people. They can provide you with solid information on your issue, additional resources, and exciting action ideas.

Globalization/Poverty

Canada World Youth
2330 Notre-Dame Street West, 3rd floor
Montréal, Québec H3J 1N4
Tel: 514-931-3526
Toll free: 1-800-605-3526
Fax: 514-939-2621
E-mail: cwy-jcm@cwy-jcm.org

Canadian International Development Agency
  (CIDA)
Communications Branch
200 Promenade du Portage
Gatineau, Québec K1A 0G4
Tel: 819-997-5456, ext. 208
Toll free: 1-800-230-6349, ext. 208
Fax: 819-953-6088
E-mail: info@bp208.ca

CorpWatch
1611 Telegraph Avenue, Suite 702
Oakland, California 94612 USA
Tel: 510-271-8080
Fax: 510-271-8083

The Council of Canadians
502-151 Slater Street
Ottawa, Ontario K1P 5H3
Tel: 613-233-2773
Toll free: 1-800-387-7177
Fax: 613-233-6776
E-mail: inquiries@canadians.org

Counterpart International
1200 18th Street NW, Suite 1100
Washington, DC 20036 USA
Tel: 202-296-9676
Fax: 202-296-9679
E-mail: communications@counterpart.org

Free the Children
7368 Yonge Street, Suite 300
Thornhill, Ontario L4J 8H9
Tel: 905-760-9382
Fax: 905-760-9157
E-mail: info@freethechildren.com

Global Change Game
P.O. Box 1632
Winnipeg, Manitoba R3C 2Z2
Tel: 204-783-2675
Fax: 204-783-2680
E-mail: gcg@mts.net

Maquila Solidarity Network
606 Shaw Street
Toronto, Ontario M6G 3L6
Tel: 416-532-8584
Fax: 416-532-7688
E-mail: info@maquilasolidarity.org

Oxfam Canada
National Office
880 Wellington Street, Suite 400
Ottawa, Ontario K1R 6K7
Tel: 613-237-5236
Fax: 613-237-0524
E-mail: enquire@oxfam.ca

Youth Challenge International
20 Maud Street, Suite 305
Toronto, Ontario M5V 2M5
Tel: 416-504-3370, ext. 300
Fax: 416-504-3376
E-mail: generalinfo@yci.org

Substance Abuse

Alcohol and Drug Concerns
1262 Don Mills Road, Suite 77
Toronto, Ontario M3B 2W7
Tel: 416-293-3400
Fax: 416-293-1142
E-mail: info@concerns.ca

Canadian Centre on Substance Abuse
75 Albert Street, Suite 300
Ottawa, Ontario K1P 5E7
Tel: 613-235-4048
Fax: 613-235-8101

Join Together
1 Appleton Street, 4th floor
Boston, Massachusetts 02116-5223 USA
Tel: 617-437-1500
Fax: 617-437-9394
E-mail: info@jointogether.org

Mothers Against Drunk Driving (MADD
  Canada)
6507C Mississauga Road
Mississauga, Ontario L5N 1A6
Tel: 905-813-6233
Toll free: 1-800-665-6233
Fax: 905-813-8920
E-mail: info@madd.ca

National Council on Alcoholism and Drug
   Dependence Inc.
20 Exchange Place, Suite 2902
New York, New York 10005 USA
Tel: 212-269-7797
Fax: 212-269-7510
E-mail: national@ncadd.org

Ontario Students Against Impaired Driving
   (OSAID)
506-5770 Hurontario Street
Mississauga, Ontario L5R 3G5
Toll free: 1-877-706-SAID
E-mail: osaid@osaid.org

SMART (Self Management and Recovery
   Training)
7537 Mentor Avenue, Suite 306
Mentor, Ohio 44060-5400 USA
Tel: 440-951-5357
Fax: 440-951-5358
E-mail: srmail1@aol.com

Students Against Destructive Decisions
SADD, Inc.
P.O. Box 800
Marlborough, Massachusetts 01752 USA
Tel: 508-481-5759
Toll free: 1-877-SADD-INC

Youth Activism Project
P.O. Box E
Kensington, Maryland 20895 USA
Tel: 1-800-KID-POWER
E-mail: info@youthactivism.com

Youth Advisory Committee on Tobacco Issues
Health Canada
A.L. 0900C2
Ottawa, Ontario K1A 0K9
Tel: 613-957-2991
Toll free: 1-800-267-1245
Fax: 613-941-5366
E-mail: YAC@hc-sc.gc.ca

Peace and Democracy

Amnesty International Canada
312 Laurier Avenue East
Ottawa, Ontario K1N 1H9
Tel: 613-744-7667
Toll free: 1-800-AMNESTY
Fax: 613-746-2411
E-mail: info@amnesty.ca

Canadian Human Rights Foundation
1425 René-Lévesque Boulevard West, Suite 407
Montréal, Québec H3G 1T7
Tel: 514-954-0382
Fax: 514-954-0659
E-mail: chrf@chrf.ca

The Canadian Peace Alliance
427 Bloor Street West, Box 13
Toronto, Ontario M5S 1X7
Tel: 416-588-5555
Fax: 416-588-5556
E-mail: cpa@web.ca

Engineers Without Borders (Canada) -
   Ingénieurs Sans Frontières (Canada)
188 Davenport Rd, 201
Toronto, Ontario M5R 1J2
Tel: 416-481-3696
Fax: 416-222-0166
E-mail: info@ewb.ca

Free the Children
7368 Yonge Street, Suite 300
Thornhill, Ontario L4J 8H9
Tel: 905-760-9382
Fax: 905-760-9157
E-mail: info@freethechildren.com

Human Rights Watch
350 Fifth Avenue, 34th floor
New York, New York 10118-3299 USA
Tel: 212-290-4700
Fax: 212-736-1300
E-mail: hrwnyc@hrw.org

Mines Action Canada
1 Nicholas Street, Suite 1502
Ottawa, Ontario K1N 7B7
Tel: 613-241-3777
Fax: 613-244-3410
E-mail: macinfo@web.ca

Seeds of Peace
370 Lexington Avenue, Suite 401
New York, New York 10017 USA
Tel: 212-573-8040
Fax: 212-573-8047
E-mail: info@seedsofpeace.org

War Child Canada
401 Richmond Street West, Studio 204
Toronto, Ontario M5V 3A8
Tel: 416-971-7471
Toll free: 1-866-WARCHILD
Fax: 416-971-7946
E-mail: info@warchild.ca

Youth for Social Justice
2099 Gottingen Street
Halifax, Nova Scotia B3N 3B3
Tel: 902-425-7877
Fax: 902-425-7778
E-mail: yfsj@hotmail.com

Child Poverty in Canada

Campaign 2000
c/o Family Service Association of Toronto
355 Church Street
Toronto, Ontario M5B 1Z8
Tel: 416-595-9230, ext. 244
Fax: 416-595-0242
E-mail: liyugu@fsatoronto.com

Canadian Council on Social Development
309 Cooper Street, 5th Floor
Ottawa, Ontario K2P 0G5
Tel: 613-236-8977
Fax: 613-236-2750
E-mail: council@ccsd.ca

Covenant House Toronto
20 Gerrard Street East
Toronto, Ontario M5B 2P3
Tel: 416-598-4898
Toll free: 1-800-HELP-308
Fax: 416-204-7030
E-mail: Cino@covenanthouse.on.ca

Daily Bread Food Bank
191 New Toronto Street
Toronto, Ontario M8V 2E7
Tel: 416-203-0050
Fax: 416-203-0049
E-mail: info@dailybread.ca

Free the Children
7368 Yonge Street, Suite 300
Thornhill, Ontario L4J 8H9
Tel: 905-760-9382
Fax: 905-760-9157
E-mail: info@freethechildren.com

National Anti-Poverty Organization
2212 Gladwin Crescent, Unit C7
Ottawa, Ontario K1B 5N1
Tel: 613-789-0096
Toll free: 1-800-810-1076
Fax: 613-789-0141
E-mail: napo@napo-onap.ca

National Council of Welfare
112 Kent Street, 9th Floor
Place de Ville, Tower B
Ottawa, Ontario K1A 0J9
Tel: 613-957-2961
Fax: 613-957-0680
E-mail: ncw@magi.com

National Youth in Care Network
99 Fifth Avenue, Suite 20
Ottawa, Ontario K1S 5K4
Tel: 613-230-8945
Youth Only Phone: 1-800-790-7074
Fax: 613-230-4383
E-mail: nd@youthincare.ca

Ontario Coalition Against Poverty
10 Britain Street
Toronto, Ontario M5A 1R6
Tel: 416-925-6939
E-mail: ocap@tao.ca

Raising the Roof
200-263 Eglinton Avenue West
Toronto, Ontario M4R 1B1
Tel: 416-481-1838
Fax: 416-481-1872
E-mail: info@raisingtheroof.org

Youth Violence and Crime

British Columbia Youth Police Network
  (BCYPN)
5325 Kincaid Street
Burnaby, BC V5G 1W2
Tel: 604-775-2113
Fax: 604-660-2960
E-mail: info@bcypn.com

Canadians Against Violence Everywhere
  Advocating its Termination (CAVEAT)
P.O. Box 26044, LMRPO
Langley, British Columbia V3A 8J2
Tel: 604-530-5829
Fax: 604-530-5831
E-mail: bc@caveat.org

The Canadian Safe School Network
111 Peter Street, Suite 617
Toronto, Ontario M5V 2H1
Tel: 416-977-1050
Fax: 905-977-9514
E-mail: info@canadiansafeschools.com

Center for the Study and Prevention of
  Violence
Institute of Behavioral Science
University of Colorado at Boulder
439 UCB Boulder, Colorado 80309-0439 USA
Tel: 303-492-8465
Fax: 303-443-3297

Empowered Student Partnership
Community Policing Unit
Toronto Police Service
40 College Street
Toronto, Ontario M5G 2J3
Tel: 416-808-7044

Leave Out ViolencE (LOVE)
National Administrative Office
3101 Bathurst Street, Unit 301
Toronto, Ontario M6A 2A6
Tel: 416-785-8411
Fax: 416-785-1236
E-mail: toronto@leaveoutviolence.com
E-mail: torontoprograms@leaveoutviolence.com

National Crime Prevention Strategy
National Crime Prevention Centre
222 Queen Street, 11th Floor
Ottawa, Ontario K1A 0H8
Tel: 613-941-9306
Toll free: 1-877-302-6272
E-mail: info@prevention.gc.ca

YouCan! Youth Canada Association
797 Somerset Street West, Suite 34
Ottawa, Ontario K1R 6R3
Tel: 613-230-1903
Toll free: 1-888-4youcan
Fax: 613-233-3700
Toll free fax: 1-877-309-5969
E-mail: info@youcan.ca

Youth Assisting Youth
401-5734 Yonge Street
Toronto, Ontario M2M 4E7
Tel: 416-932-1919
Toll free: 1-877-932-1919
Fax: 416-932-1924
E-mail: mail@yay.org

Youth Crime Watch of America
9200 South Dadeland Boulevard, Suite 417
Miami, Florida 33156 USA
Tel: 305-670-2409
Fax: 305-670-3805
E-mail: ycwa@ycwa.org

Sustainable Consumption and the Environment

Canadian Wildlife Federation
350 Michael Cowpland Drive
Kanata, Ontario K2M 2W1
Tel: 613-599-9594
Toll free: 1-800-563-WILD
Fax: 613-599-4428
E-mail: info@cwf-fcf.org

EarthYouth
c/o Taking IT Global
42 Charles Street East
Toronto, Ontario M4Y 1T4
Tel: 416-928-3362. ext. 4225
E-mail: earthyouth@earthyouth.net

Eco-Males and Females In Action (eco-Mafia)
c/o UWSA
515 Portage Avenue
Winnipeg, Manitoba R3B 2E9
Tel: 204-786-9189
E-mail: ecomafia@yahoo.com

Jane Goodall Institute Canada
5165 Sherbrooke Street West, Suite 301
Montréal, Québec H4A 1T6
Tel: 514-369-3384
Toll Free: 1-888-88-CHIMP
Fax: 514-489-8748
E-mail: info@janegoodall.ca

The Otesha Project
20 Banting Crescent
Kanata, Ontario K2K 1P4
Tel: 613-591-3607
E-mail: info@otesha.ca

Sierra Youth Coalition
SYC National Office
1 Nicholas Street, Suite 412
Ottawa, ON K1N 7B7
Tel: 613-241-1615
Toll free: 1-888-790-7393
Fax: 613-241-2292
E-mail: info@syc-cjs.org

Toronto Environmental Alliance
30 Duncan Street, Suite 201
Toronto, Ontario M5V 2C3
Tel: 416-596-0660
Fax: 416-596-0345
E-mail: tea@torontoenvironment.org

WaterCan
321 Chapel Street
Ottawa, Ontario K1N 7Z2
Tel: 613-230-5182
Toll free: 1-800-370-5658
Fax: 613-230-0712
E-mail: info@watercan.com

World Wildlife Fund of Canada
245 Eglinton Avenue East, Suite 410
Toronto, Ontario M4P 3J1
Tel: 416-489-8800
Toll free: 1-800-26-PANDA
Fax: 416-489-8055
E-mail: panda@wwfcanada.org

Youth Action Effecting Change
119 West Pender, Suite 517
Vancouver, British Columbia V6B 1S5
Tel: 604-801-5752
Fax: 604-689-4242
E-mail: yaec@eya.ca

Racism

Anti-Defamation League
Department DJ
823 United Nations Plaza
New York, New York 10017 USA
Tel: 212-885-7700
E-mail: webmaster@adl.org

Anti-Racist Action Canada
P.O. Box 291, Station B
Toronto, Ontario M5T 2T2
Tel: 416-631-8835
E-mail: ara@web.net

Artists Against Racism
Box 54511
Toronto, Ontario M5M 4N5
Tel: 416-410-5631
E-mail: aar@idirect.com

Canadian Race Relations Foundation
4576 Yonge Street, Suite 701
Toronto, Ontario M2N 6N4
Tel: 416-952-3500
Toll free: 1-888-240-4936
Fax: 416-952-3326
E-mail: info@crr.ca

Colours of Resistance
c/o Student-Worker Solidarity
QPIRG at McGill
3647 University Street, 3rd Floor
Montréal, Québec H3A 2B3
E-mail: cor@mutualaid.org

Harmony Movement
255 Duncan Mill Road, Suite 412
Toronto, Ontario M3B 3H9
Tel: 416-385-2660
Fax: 416-385-2644
E-mail: info@harmony.ca

National Conference for Community and
  Justice
475 Park Avenue South, 19th Floor
New York, New York 10016 USA
Tel: 212-545-1300
Fax: 212-545-8053

World Against Racism Foundation
1826 R Street Northwest
Washington, District of Columbia 20009
  USA
Tel: 202-462-0808
Fax: 202-462-0807
E-mail: webmaster@endracism.com

Youth Against Racism
Multicultural Association of Nova Scotia
1113 Marginal Road
Halifax, Nova Scotia B3H 4P7
Tel: 902-423-6534
Fax: 902-422-0881
E-mail: lisa@Mans.ns.ca

Youth Forums Against Racism
Tel: 613-232-5751, ext. 249/240
E-mail: yfar@unac.org

Exploitation of Children

Beyond Borders — Ensuring Global Justice
  for Children
387 Broadway Avenue
Winnipeg, Manitoba R3C 0V5
Tel: 204-284-6862
Fax: 204-452-1333
Email: rprober@beyondborders.org

Canadian Coalition for the Rights of Children
c/o Canadian Child Care Federation
201-383 Parkdale Avenue
Ottawa, Ontario K1Y 4R4
E-mail: info@rightsofchildren.ca

The Children's Defense Fund
25 E Street NW
Washington, District of Columbia 20001
  USA
Tel: 202-628-8787
E-mail: cdfinfo@childrensdefense.org

Free the Children
7368 Yonge Street, Suite 300
Thornhill, Ontario L4J 8H9
Tel: 905-760-9382
Fax: 905-760-9157
E-mail: info@freethechildren.com

Global Children's Organization
Box 67583
9911 Pico Boulevard
Los Angeles, California 90067 USA
Tel: 310-581-2234
Fax: 310-934-0308
E-mail: gco@globalchild.org

International Bureau for Children's Rights
1185 Saint-Mathieu Street
Montréal, Québec H3H 2P7
Tel: 514-932-7656
Fax: 514-932-9453
E-mail: info@ibcr.org

Save the Children Canada
National Office
4141 Yonge Street, Suite 300
Toronto, Ontario M2P 2A8
Tel: 416-221-5501
Toll free: 1-800-668-5036
Fax: 416-221-8214
E-mail: sccan@savethechildren.ca

Students Against Sweatshops — Canada
c/o OPIRG Toronto
563 Spadina Ave, Room 101
Toronto, Ontario M5S 2J7
Tel: 416-978-7770
Fax: 416-971-2292
E-mail: opirg@campuslife.utoronto.ca

UNICEF Canada
Canada Square
2200 Yonge Street, Suite 1100
Toronto, Ontario M4S 2C6
Tel: 416-482-4444
Fax: 416-482-8035
E-mail: secretary@unicef.ca

Youth Advocate Program International
4545 42nd Street NW, Suite 209
Washington, District of Columbia 20016
  USA
Tel: 202-244-1986
Fax: 202-244-6396
E-mail: yapi@yapi.org

Aboriginal Rights

The Aboriginal Rights Coalition
National Office, ARC Ottawa
153 Laurier Avenue East
Ottawa, Ontario K1N 6N8
Tel: 613-235-9956
E-mail: arc@istar.ca

Aboriginal Youth Council
c/o National Association of Friendship
  Centres
275 MacLaren Street
Ottawa, Ontario K2P 0L9
Tel: 613-563-4844
Fax: 613-594-3428

The Aboriginal Youth Network
Box 34007 Kingsway PO
Edmonton, AB T5G 3G4
Tel: 780-459-1058
Toll free: 1-866-459-1058
Fax: 780-419-7266
E-mail: siteadmin@ayn.ca

All Indian Pueblo Council
2401 12th Street Northwest
Albuquerque, New Mexico 87104 USA
Tel: 505-975-4094/4100
Fax: 505-883-7682

Assembly of First Nations
1 Nicholas Street, Suite 1002
Ottawa, Ontario K1N 7B7
Tel: 613-241-6789
Fax: 613-241-5808

The Gathering Place
P.O. Box 838
23 First Street
Thoreau, New Mexico 87323 USA
Tel: 505-862-8075
Toll free: 1-800-862-5763
Fax: 505-862-8809
E-mail: gathplac@cia-g.com

Inuit Tapiriit of Canada
170 Laurier Street West, Suite 510
Ottawa, Ontario K1P 5V5
Tel: 613-238-8181
Fax: 613-234-1991

Native American Rights Fund
1506 Broadway
Boulder, Colorado 80302 USA
Tel: 303-447-8760
Fax: 303-443-7776

The Native American Women's Health
  Education Resource Center
P.O. Box 572
Lake Andes, South Dakota 57356 USA
Tel: 605-487-7072
Fax: 605-487-7964
E-mail: nativewoman@igc.apc.org

Ojibway & Cree Cultural Centre
273 Third Avenue, Suite 204
Timmins, Ontario P4N 1E2
Tel: 705-267-7911
Fax: 705-267-4988
E-mail: info@occc.ca

HIV/AIDS

AIDS Committee of Toronto
399 Church Street, 4th Floor
Toronto, Ontario M5B 2J6
Tel: 416-340-AIDS or 416-340-8484
Fax: 416-340-8224
E-mail: communications@actoronto.org

A Loving Spoonful
1300 Richards Street, Suite 100
Vancouver, British Columbia V6B 3G6
Tel: 604-682-6325
Fax: 604-682-6327
E-mail: info@alovingspoonful.org

Canadian Aboriginal AIDS Network
602-251 Bank Street
Ottawa, Ontario K2P 1X3
Tel: 613-567-1817
Toll free: 1-888-285-2226
Fax: 613-567-4652
E-mail: info@caan.ca

Canadian AIDS Treatment Information
  Exchange
555 Richmond Street West, Suite 505
Box 1104
Toronto, Ontario M5V 3B1
Tel: 416-203-7122
Toll free: 1-800-263-1638
Fax: 416-203-8284
E-mail: info@catie.ca

Canadian Working Group on HIV and
  Rehabilitation
333 Sherbourne Street
Toronto, Ontario M5A 2S5
Tel: 416-324-4182
Fax: 416-324-4184
E-mail: cwghr@hivandrehab.ca

Farha Foundation
7080 Parc Avenue, Suite 10
Montréal, Québec H3N 1X6
Tel: 514-270-4900
Fax: 514-270-5363
E-mail: farha@farha.qc.ca

Fife House
571 Jarvis Street
Toronto, Ontario M4Y 2J1
Tel: 416-205-9888
Fax: 416-205-9919
E-mail: info@fifehouse.org

UNAIDS
20 Avenue Appia
CH-1211 Geneva 27
Switzerland
Tel: +41-22-791-3666
Fax: +41-22-791-4187
E-mail: unaids@unaids.org

World Health Organization
525 23rd Street NW
Washington, DC 20037 USA
Tel: 202-974-3000
Fax: 202-974-3663
E-mail: postmaster@paho.org

YouthCO AIDS Society
1104 Hornby Street, Suite 205
Vancouver, British Columbia V6Z 1V8
Tel: 604-688-1441
Toll free: 1-877-YouthCO
Fax: 604-688-4932
E-mail: information@youthco.org

A Final Word

Being a global citizen is not always easy. There will be times when you lose hope, especially when you are dealing with complex issues such as war, environmental degradation, or poverty in inner city communities. It is easy to feel that nothing you do will make a difference. After all, you are just one person. What difference can you make?

We learned the answer to this question not long after we first became involved in social justice issues. We were attending an international youth conference where thousands of young people had gathered to learn about the challenges our world faces and brainstorm ways to help. By the last day, we felt inspired by what we had learned from one another but also worried that our action plans would be too small to overcome the world's enormous problems — that they wouldn't make a dent.

For the closing ceremonies of the conference, all the participants gathered in the quiet stadium. One young person stood in the centre of the room, holding a lit candle, and called out the one question that was on all of our minds:

"I am one person. What difference can I make?"

She then turned to the four people closest to her, and lit the candles in their hands. Those four walked out to the corners of the stadium, repeated the question, and each lit the candles of five people they met there. The same question was echoed by the group fifteen times, and each time, the flame was passed forward. In this way, the firelight spread from one person to thousands until finally every candle was lit, and the whole stadium was aglow.

It was a simple but powerful statement. While it may seem naïve, it's important to recognize that every major social change comes about in this way, through very small, simple actions that spread like wildfire.

As an informed and inspired global citizen, be the first one to light the flame. A better world begins with you.

About Free the Children

Free the Children is a unique international youth organization that empowers young people through representation, leadership, and action. Founded in 1995 by then 12-year-old Craig Kielburger, Free the Children has grown into the world's largest network of children helping children, having involved more than one million young people around the world in its projects.

Over 130 million of the world's poorest children do not attend school, and two thirds of them are girls. Because education is the best way to end poverty and the exploitation of children, Free the Children has raised funds to build more than 375 schools in 23 developing countries, providing daily education to over 30 000 children. Free the Children young people have also collected and shipped 200 000 school and health kits and more than 8 million Can$ in medical supplies to children in 40 countries of the developing world. These countries include Afghanistan, Sierra Leone, Ecuador, India, China, Kosovo, Kenya, Togo, Brazil, Haiti, Nicaragua, Tanzania, Mexico, and the Philippines,

among others. Alternative income-generating programs sponsored by Free the Children empower poor families, and especially poor women, with the means to send their children to school.

As a voice for young people, Free the Children takes a stand on children's rights issues on local, national, and international levels. Youth representatives address students, educators, unions, religious groups, businesses, and government groups on social issues affecting children.

Free the Children is a group of passionate young people from all ages who wish to change the world! There are many ways for you, your school, or youth group to become involved and make a difference in the lives of children around the globe:

- Start a Free the Children chapter in your school.

- Fundraise to build a classroom or a school in a developing country.

- Research important issues such as child labour, children in armed conflict, and child poverty in Canada, and educate others about what they can do to help.

- Participate in a Free the Children campaign for children's rights.

- Attend one of Free the Children's leadership academies and conferences, which take place in Toronto and Arizona each year.

Visit www.freethechildren.com for more information on how to become involved, including how to start a Free the Children chapter, fundraising ideas, fact sheets on important global issues, and profiles of youth who have changed the world.

About Leaders Today

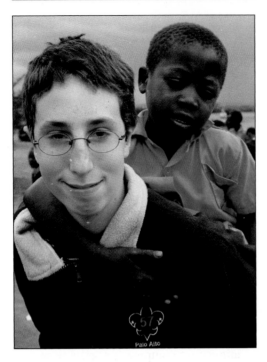

Young people are not only the leaders of tomorrow; they are also the leaders of today! Leaders Today believes that leadership development is the key to achieving a generation of committed and socially active young people. Founded by Marc and Craig Kielburger in 1999, Leaders Today educates and empowers tens of thousands of young people around the world each year with the skills to become active global citizens.

Leaders Today offers unique programs to unlock the leadership potential of all young people, including:

- *International Volunteer Opportunities:* Leaders Today organizes and facilitates global volunteer trips to Kenya, Ecuador, Nicaragua, Mexico, India, and Thailand. Trip highlights include constructing a primary school, teaching English, leadership seminars, language lessons, and building lifelong friendships.

- *International Leadership and Volunteer Centres:* Leaders Today has two leadership and volunteer centres that accept school or religious groups and volunteers throughout the academic year. Located in the Masai Mara region of Kenya and in Patagonia, Arizona, the centres provide ideal volunteerism and leadership opportunities.

- *Leadership Academies:* Leaders Today offers leadership academies during the summer and March Break in Toronto, Ontario, and Patagonia, Arizona, where participants take part in intensive one-week leadership training programs, including facilitator training courses.

- *Global Leadership Programs:* Leaders Today facilitators can come to your school, conference, or place of worship to teach leadership skills such as effective public speaking, team building, working with the media, fundraising, and more.

- *Motivational Speakers and Speaking Tours:* Leaders Today has world-class youth motivational speakers who are ideal for youth-related gatherings or events.

- *School Board Partnerships:* Leaders Today works with many of the largest school boards across North America to administer leadership programs and co-ordinate volunteer initiatives.

Visit www.leaderstoday.com for more information on how you can gain the skills, confidence, and experiences to change the world.

Glossary

agenda a list or plan of things to be discussed or accomplished

branding the act of giving a company or organization a particular design or symbol in order to promote its products, services, or message

bridge-builders leaders who negotiate to resolve conflicts between members to ensure that the team stays focused and works as a cohesive unit

budget an estimate of the amount of money that will be spent for various purposes in a given time

citizen one who is granted specific rights and responsibilities as a member of a state or nation

contingency funds money put aside to cover unexpected costs

Core Group three to five passionate and committed people who work together to plan and co-ordinate research and actions for an issue, making it a high priority in their lives

doers leaders who take action to set the team in motion, leading by example, motivating people toward the main goal

ecological footprint all the productive land required on a continuing basis to provide all the resources consumed and absorb all the wastes created by a population, no matter where in the world that land is located; how much of Earth was affected in the production and the eventual disposal of a particular product

ethical being in accordance with standards of right and wrong

facilitator one who is responsible for ensuring that group members treat one another with respect and follow the agenda during meetings; a facilitator may also encourage group interaction

global citizen one who considers the global impact of one's words and actions, questions the status quo, strives for a more just and sustainable world, and celebrates diversity and solidarity

global citizenship the responsibilities, rights, and privileges of being a member of the global community

globalization the increased mobility of goods, services, labour, technology, and capital throughout the world

HTML acronym for Hypertext Markup Language, a computer programming language used to create and display hypertext files (from which text, graphics, and sound can be accessed by selecting a specially marked word on the screen) on the Internet

Java a computer programming language designed to develop applications, especially ones for the Internet that can operate on different platforms

lobbying trying to influence people, especially legislators

media outlets businesses or companies focused on communicating news and events to the public, such as newspapers, magazines, and television and radio stations

metatag a Hypertext Markup Language (HTML) command that defines keywords within Web documents (*see also* HTML)

Minga Team a group of occasional volunteers who contribute their talents to the team during big actions; a term inspired by the indigenous societies in Central and South America who come together to accomplish important projects quickly, efficiently, and as a unified community

mission the particular objective of a group

mission statement a written outline of the group's objective

monitoring and evaluation plans materials prepared before an action, including feedback forms, surveys, and tallies, that allow a group to measure its success in quantity and in quality

networking meeting with friends or colleagues to exchange ideas or further one's interests

passion booster a visible, tangible reminder of one's mission, which stirs memory and rekindles passion about an issue

prayer in a petition, what is being requested

press kits a packaged set of promotional materials, such as photographs and background information, for distribution to the press, as at a news conference

public service announcements (PSAs) advertisements or commercials promoting a social message and broadcast on radio and television stations

racism prejudice or discrimination against a person or group because of a difference of race or of cultural or ethnic background

reasoners leaders who analyse the team's goals and actions, and determine the best possible way to achieve the goals, given specific conditions and circumstances

search engines a piece of software used to find and access files or Web sites; examples include Google, Lycos, MSN, and Yahoo

site map a visual or textually organized model of a Web site's content that allows the users to navigate through the site to find the information they are looking for; a kind of interactive table of contents, in which each listed item links directly to its counterpart sections of the Web site

solidarity unity or fellowship arising from common responsibilities and interests

sound bite a short, catchy phrase or slogan that communicates a group's message

status quo the way things are; the existing state of affairs

substance abuse excessive use of a drug, alcohol, or other chemical agent that may lead to social, occupational, psychological, or physical problems

sustainable consumption meeting your needs with minimal negative social and environmental impacts, while maximizing positive impacts; actions that meet your needs without sacrificing the needs of future generations

thesis in a speech, a proposition or statement to be proved or to be maintained against objections

values beliefs that individuals or groups hold about what is really important or just, and that guide choices and behaviour

visionaries leaders who dream of the team's goals and potential; those who develop new ideas for approaching problems or tasks

Select Bibliography

Campaign 2000, "Poverty Amidst Prosperity: Campaign 2000–2002 Report Card on Child and Family Poverty." http://www.campaign2000.ca/rc/rc02/intro.html (Jan. 6, 2004)

Dingerson, Leigh and Hay, Sarah H. *Co/Motion: The Guide to Youth-Led Social Change.* Washington DC: Alliance for Justice, 1998.

Health Canada, "The Scoop." http://www.hc-sc.gc.ca/hecs-sesc/tobacco/youth/scoop.html#never (Jan. 7, 2004)

Human Rights Watch, "Racism and the Administration of Justice." http://www.hrw.org/campaigns/race/criminal_justice.htm (Jan. 7, 2004)

Human Rights Watch, "Unfair Advantage: Workers' Freedom of Association in the US Under International Human Rights Standards." http://www.hrw.org/reports/2000/uslabor/ (Jan. 7, 2004)

Human Rights Watch, "World Conference Against Racism Backgrounder." http://www.hrw.org/campaigns/race/background0727.htm (Jan. 7, 2004)

Indian and Northern Affairs Canada, "Aboriginal People in Canada and the Federal Budget." http://www.ainc-inac.gc.ca/nr/prs/j-a2000/mar7bk_e.html (Jan. 12, 2004)

International Institute for Democracy and Electoral Assistance, "Participation, Political Parties and Institutions." http://www.idea.int/thematic_b.htm (Jan. 7, 2004)

International Labour Organization, "Johannesburg Summit 2002: World Summit on Sustainable Development." http://www.ilo.org/public/english/bureau/inf/wssd/index.htm (Jan. 7, 2004)

International Rehabilitation Council for Torture Victims, "About Torture." http://www.irct.org/usr/irct/home.nsf/unid/JREW-5GHJL2 (Jan. 7, 2004)

Jones, Ellis et al. *The Better World Handbook: From Good Intentions to Everyday Actions.* Gabriola Island, BC: New Society Publishers, 2001.

Kahn, Si. *Organizing: a Guide for Grassroots Leaders.* Silver Spring, MD: National Association of Social Workers, 1991.

Kidder, Rushworth M., "The Eagle and the Knapsack." http://www.josephsoninstitute.org/poc/cleland.htm (Feb. 12, 2003)

King Jr., Martin Luther, "I Have a Dream." http://news.bbc.co.uk/1/hi/world/americas/3170387.stm (Jan. 6, 2004)

MADD Canada, "The Real Facts on Alcohol Use, Injuries and Deaths." http://www.madd.ca/library/madd_alcohol_facts.pdf (Jan. 7, 2004)

Mandela, Nelson, "I Am Prepared to Die." www.anc.org.za.ancdocs/history/mandela/1960s/rivonia.html (Mar. 8, 2002)

Myers, David G. *Social Psychology*, 7th ed. New York: McGraw-Hill, 2002.

The Native Women's Association of Canada, "Discrimination Against Aboriginal Women Rampant in Federal Prisons, Claims the Native Women's Association of Canada." http://www.elizabethfry.ca/submissn/prelease/nwac/nwac.pdf (Jan. 7, 2004)

Oxfam Quebec, "The Right to Life and Security." http://www.oxfam.qc.ca/html_en/programs/droit3_vie_en.html (Jan. 7, 2004)

Rainforest Action Network, "Rates of Rainforest Lost." http://www.ran.org/info_center/factsheets/04b.html (Jan. 7, 2004)

Rose, Thomas, "Hafsat Abiola Shares Passion With Students." http://horizon.westmont.edu/horizon01/11_27_01/news/story4.shtml (Jan. 6, 2004)

Statistics Canada, "Canadian Centre for Justice Statistics Profile Series: Children and Youth in Canada." http://www.statcan.ca/english/freepub/85F0033MIE/85F0033MIE01005.pdf (Jan. 9, 2004)

Stockholm International Peace Research Institute, "Global Military Spending Perspective." http://projects.sipri.se/milex/mex_trends.html (Jan. 10, 2004)

UNAIDS, "UNICEF and UNAIDS Applaud Milestone in Forging Coordinated Global Response to Growing Crisis of Children Orphaned Due to AIDS." www.unaids.org/html/pub/Media/Press-Releases01/ Joint_pressrelease_UNICEF_21Oct03_en_pdf.pdf (Jan. 7, 2004)

UNESCO Institute for Statistics, "Literacy." http://www.uis.unesco.org/ev.php?URL_ID=4926&URL_DO=DO_TOPIC&URL_SECTION=201 (Jan. 10, 2004)

UNICEF, "A League Table of Child Poverty in Rich Nations." http://www.unicef-icdc.org/publications/pdf/repcard1e.pdf (Jan. 6, 2004)

UNICEF, "The State of the World's Children 1999: Education." http://www.unicef.org/sowc99/ (Jan. 10, 2004)

United Nations, "Universal Declaration of Human Rights." www.un.org/rights/50/decla/htm (Mar. 8, 2002)

United Nations Office on Drugs and Crime, "Trafficking in Human Beings." http://www.unodc.org/unodc/trafficking_human_beings.html (Jan. 7, 2004)

Welton, Neva and Wolf, Linda. *Global Uprising: Confronting the Tyrannies of the 21st Century.* Gabriola Island, BC: New Society Publishers, 2001.

World Health Organization, "AIDS Epidemic Update: December 2002." http://www.who.int/hiv/pub/epidemiology/epi2002/en/ (Jan. 7, 2004)

World Summit of Sustainable Development, Johannesburg 2002, "Facts about Consumption and Production Patterns." http://www.johannesburgsummit.org/html/media_info/pressreleases_factsheets/wssd9_consumption.pdf (January 8, 2004)